Choosing & Caring For a Shelter Dog

A COMPLETE GUIDE TO HELP YOU RESCUE & REHOME A DOG

BOB CHRISTIANSEN

CANINE LEARNING CENTER
PUBLISHING DIVISION
NAPA, CALIFORNIA

Printed in the United States of America

Published by

Canine Learning Center — Publishing Division

P.O. Box 10515, Napa, CA 94581

For orders please call: **1-800-354-DOGS** (1-800-354-3647)

e-mail: k9learning@aol.com

Publisher's Cataloging in Publication Data

Christiansen, Bob.

Choosing a shelter dog: a complete guide to help you rescue & rehome a dog / Bob Christiansen.

p. cm.

1. Dogs. 2. Pets. 3. Animal shelters. I. Title.

SF426.C47 1996 636.7'087 QBI96-20228

Library of Congress Catalog Card No. 96-084319

ISBN 1-884421-55-5

Limit of Liability/Disclaimer of Warranty

Discounts

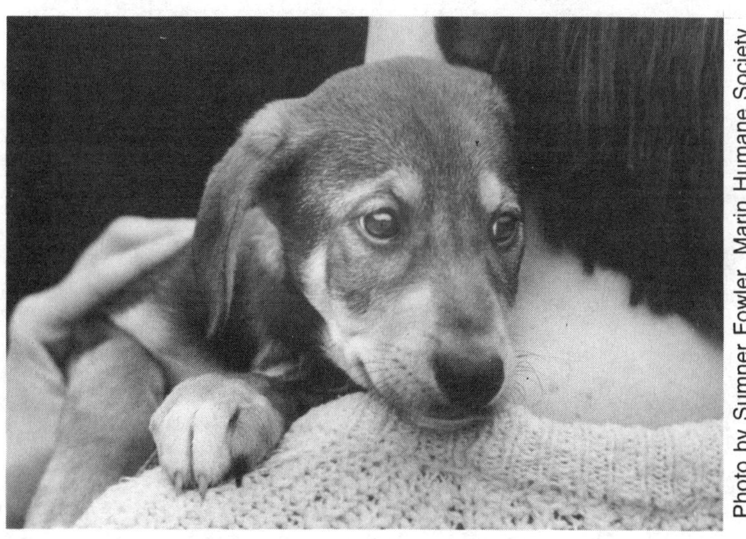

Photo by Sumner Fowler, Marin Humane Society

This book is dedicated to all those who work to rescue and rehome orphaned dogs

Acknowledgments

I would like to thank all those animal-care professionals who have helped contribute to this book. Their technical assistance, knowledge and advice have been invaluable in putting forth this publication. Darris Hercs, Assistant Executive Director, Oakland SPCA; Christine Arnold, Executive Director, Humane Society of Santa Clara Valley; Mary Lee Geyer, Santa Cruz SPCA; Julia Fishel, Los Angeles SPCA/Southern California Humane Society; Steve McNall, Executive Director, Pasadena Humane Society; Mike Kaufman, American Humane Association; Ann Wilde, Kaci Anderson, Helen Hamilton, Consultant; Marcia Wigdahl, Trainer & Behaviorist; Candace Schuman, Chairperson, Spay/Neuter Action Project; Roxanne Hawn, American Animal Hospital Association; Laura Restivo, SPCA of Texas and Gary Patronek, M.S., V.M.D. Special thanks to Julie Miller and Rachael Lamb of the Humane Society of the United States.

Veterinary editing by Dr. David Zanders, DVM Westward Bernardo; Dr. Robert Cartin, DVM Mission Animal Hospital; Dr. Michael Mulvany, DVM, and Jean Hamilton, All Creatures Animal Hospital; Dr. Gary Rose, Cabrillo Animal Hospital; and Pauline White, San Diego County Veterinary Medical Association.

Typesetting and design: Word Wizards®, Oceanside, California

Photos by: Sumner Fowler, Marin Humane Society, David Jensen, Alaska Pet-ography and Click, the Photo Connection

Cover dog: **Bandit** had four homes in his first two years and came close to losing his life. Fortunately, he was discovered by Helen Hamilton of San Diego, California, with whom he has lived happily for the last eight years.

Thank You for Caring About a Dog's Life

Dogs are one of the greatest pleasures in life. They give us unconditional loyalty and acceptance, provide constant companionship and help relieve the stress of everyday living. There are many advantages to dog ownership. There is no doubt this special relationship enriches our lives. Unfortunately, not everyone is able to achieve the human / animal bond and many animals are homeless. In most cases, the bond never had a chance to develop and mature. Researchers tell us, "Adults who retain their pets have strong ***reasonable expectations*** for the roles pets will play in their own lives and the lives of their children, and therefore develop strong attachments to their pets." In order to successfully adopt a shelter dog, you must know ahead of time what you are getting yourself into. You must carefully plan and be prepared for the responsibility and commitment of ownership.

This book is a helpful, all-inclusive guide for those special people who are considering or are currently rehoming an abandoned dog. Every major facet of selecting, training and caring for a shelter dog is at your fingertips. This book will help you understand a shelter dog's behavior and help you achieve a satisfying relationship, especially if you are a first-time adopter inexperienced with the unique needs of shelter dogs. Most dog owners have the best intentions when they obtain a dog. However, frustrations can develop and lead to anger, neglect and abandonment. Don't let that happen to you! Your dog's life can depend on it!

If you are currently searching for a dog, please include a trip to your local shelter. You will be pleasantly surprised to find the wonderful dogs that are available, and you can enjoy the added benefit of knowing your effort of adopting a dog has saved a dog's life.

Photo by Alaska Pet-ography

Ten Things a Dog Asks of Its Family

1. My life is likely to last 10 to 15 years. Any permanent separation from you will be painful for me. Remember that before you obtain me.
2. Do not break my spirit with harsh treatment. Your patience and understanding will more quickly teach me the things you would have me learn.
3. Teach me how you want me to behave. I want to please you, but I need to know how. It's crucial for my well-being.
4. Don't be angry with me for long, and do not lock me up as a punishment. You have your work, your entertainment and your friends. I only have you and I like being with you.
5. Talk to me. Even if I don't understand your words I understand the tone of your voice when you are speaking to me, especially when you use friendly tones.
6. Be aware that I am normally a social animal; however, I need to make positive associations at a young age to feel confident and well-adjusted around other dogs and humans.
7. Remember I need activity, both mental and physical. I enjoy playing games, taking walks and going on a good run.
8. Before you scold me for being uncooperative, obstinate or lazy, ask yourself if something may be bothering me. Perhaps I am not getting the right food. I may be bored. I may need medical attention or I may be getting old. Keep in mind I respond very well to praise and attention.
9. Take care of me when I get old; you, too, will grow old.
10. Remember that I only want to love and please you, so treat me kindly. No heart is more grateful.

Contents

Photo by Sumner Fowler, Marin Humane Society

1

Preparing for Your Dog

Things to Consider Before You Bring a Dog Home

1. The decision to acquire a dog should be considered by all members of the family. Everyone should ask themselves, "Why do I want a dog?" If your goal is to have a good, well-trained home-obedient dog that would make an excellent family companion, then your search should definitely begin at your local shelter.

   There is a large selection from which to choose. Typically, 25% are purebred, 75% are mixed breeds, 15% are puppies. Most are under 18 months of age, all shapes, colors and sizes. These dogs make wonderful pets, as many proud adopters can testify.

   Unfortunately, only 14% of the people who acquire a pet obtain one from a shelter. Researchers tell us the major reasons. Some people do not realize their local shelter is a good source for dogs. Some believe these dogs to be of inferior quality. Some become depressed by the thought of the visit and avoid it. Some want a dog with a champion pedigree or papers. (Registration papers are necessary to participate in purebred activities. "Papers" are only a birth certificate. They do not ensure the dog's health or temperament.)

   The simple fact is most shelter dogs are good dogs. They happen to be victims of circumstance. Every search for a good canine companion for the home should start with a visit to the local shelter — you would be surprised!

2. The potential adopter needs to know the typical behaviors expected from the breed or breed mixes they want to adopt. What type of dog will you choose? Each breed was bred for certain functions and all have different exercise, training, and grooming requirements. Mixed-breed dogs usually have a prominent look, such as a shepherd mix or corgi mix. Use the breed characteristics to determine the right size, weight, coat and temperament to fit your family. The trick in selecting a dog is to know what to expect from the typical behavior of the dog you favor and to match those characteristics and behaviors with your family's life style and living situation.
3. How will you teach the dog the rules of the house? Chewing, barking, digging and house soiling are normal dog behaviors. Dogs often continue these behaviors until effectively trained. Can your family accept this and be patient, kind and consistent during the teaching process? Are you committed to working out problems when they occur? Training should start the moment you bring the dog into the home. Everyone in the household should train the dog, not just the primary care giver. Every person must be consistent.
4. Do you have enough time and energy for daily activities? Dogs require food, water, exercise, care and companionship every day of every year of their life. Surveys indicate the average owners spend two hours a day to feed, train, groom, play, exercise and clean up after their pets. Will you provide the time or will it become an annoyance or burden?
5. Have you considered the costs involved in caring for a dog, like a license, food, training, equipment, grooming supplies, toys and medical care that includes spay/neuter surgery? (Minimum $300 per year.)
6. If you are a parent, is the sole reason you want a dog to teach your preschool or grade school child to be a responsible, loving and emotionally sensitive person? Are you looking for a pet "toy" for your child? Researchers tell us there are many dogs returned to the shelter because, "It just did not work out." Be realistic. It is a job for adults.

   According to researchers Kidd, Kidd and George, "The responsibility for and caretaking of pets usually becomes the mother's obligation regardless of initial plans. Therefore, where parents expect the pet to teach the child responsibility and caretaking and the child does not learn and display these behaviors, the parents usually regret adopting the pet and frequently reject or abandon it" (*Psychological Reports*, 1992, **70**, 547-561).

Photo by Click, the Photo Connection

Children can and will benefit from an association with a dog. Studies have also shown that the relationship between children and parents was better in pet owning families and this led to a happier family atmosphere. However, children cannot be counted on to assume all of the dog's primary needs. They must be taught over time. They must learn to be respectful of the dog and SHARE in the everyday walks, feeding, cleaning up, training, playing and grooming.

If you are a parent, make sure YOU want this dog and YOU are ready to assume the responsibilities and YOU are willing and able to provide for the dog's needs. Your actions will become a model that will teach children responsibility, commitment and how to nurture a living creature.

7. Do you have permission from your landlord, preferably in writing? In San Francisco, less than 20% of rental units accept dogs. Do you know the condo rules regarding pets? What will you do if you have to move? Will you make the commitment to take the dog with you?
8. Do you have enough space to house the dog properly? How will you keep the dog under control? Certain dogs are better equipped for life in a large suburban home than in an apartment. Free-roaming dogs are a nuisance to neighbors, endanger the dog and usually are against the law. It's very cruel to chain a dog in a confined area. It often leads to behavior problems.
9. Will you mind the constant fight to control hair shedding, fleas and odors, or will they annoy and burden you? Do you, your friends or relatives have an allergic reaction to pet hair?

10. Will you be a responsible pet owner by providing vaccinations, identification, prompt health care, obeying leash laws and spaying or neutering your pet?
11. How will your pet be cared for when you go on vacation? Do you have a friend or relative you can rely on? Many dogs that are left with inexperienced caretakers end up in shelters. Can you afford the expense of a boarding kennel or pet sitter?
12. Are you committed to keep and care for your dog its entire lifetime, even when you move and your life style changes?

Dog Facts

Thirty percent of dogs are obtained from breeders, 25% from friends, 14% from animal shelters, 8% from pet stores, 23% from other sources. There are 52.3 million dogs that live in the U.S., 36.5% of all households own dogs, 1.5 dogs average per household. As many as 81% would like to have them. The primary care giver of the family pet is the female head of household, 66%, followed by the male, 19%. Half of care givers are between 30 and 50 years of age. Approximately 54% of the dogs are purebred, 46% mixed breed. Each year approximately 4.7 million dogs are euthanized in shelters. That means one every 6.7 seconds. Countless more are euthanized in veterinary offices. Of the estimated 52.3 million dogs, a little less than 15% end up in shelters. Fifty-six percent are strays, 44% are surrendered. Approximately 60% of all dogs entering shelters are euthanized, 15% reclaimed, 25% adopted nationally. One out of four dogs born finds a permanent home. Of the people who adopt shelter animals, 79% take home pets younger than 6 months of age. Of animals turned in to shelters, 42.2% are owned less than 6 months, 22.2% are owned from 6 to 12 months. Typically, only 16% of dogs are over 1 year of age when acquired. Seventy-nine percent of pet owners own dogs, 57% cats, 13% birds, 3% reptiles.

1990 Gallup Poll "Pet Census" Revealed:

Six of ten people believe people with pets lead a more satisfying life than those without them. Only 2% think pets detract from life. Eighty-eight percent said they consider their pet a member of the family. Seventy percent say they have a great deal of affection for their pet. Sixty-one percent say they miss their pet when away from it for a long period of time. Forty-one percent say they talk often to their pet. Thirty-six percent of households allow their dog on the furniture. Seventy percent of dog owners keep their dog inside at night.

Photo by Click, the Photo Connection

Scientific Research on Pet Adoptions

A 1992 study published in *Psychological Reports*, (**70**, 547-561), "Successful and Unsuccessful Pet Adoptions," by Robert Kidd, Aline Kidd and Carol George examined the issue of pet relinquishment.

The findings of their study support the theory that well-prepared owners who are able to devote time to nurture and train their pets make the most successful adopters. Their research indicated first-time pet owners were less likely to understand the money, time and nurturing requirements pet ownership demands. They concluded, "First-time pet owners did not anticipate undesirable behaviors in their newly adopted pets and they were not aware of successful techniques in coping with or eliminating them." The authors went on to say, "Lack of information about species-specific behaviors in the newly acquired pet, methods of training desirable behaviors, amount of actual time needed for good caretaking, expenses, and adopter's willingness to work out all such ownership problems wherever possible are critical factors for successful adoptions."

Choosing and Caring for a Shelter Dog

Animal Overpopulation

Overpopulation is the number one problem faced by sheltering agencies today. The blame for this needless suffering lies with people who fail to live up to their responsibilities of dog ownership and care. They allow companion animals to multiply far beyond the capacity of society to adequately provide for them. In seven years, one unspayed female and her unspayed descendants can theoretically produce 4,372 more dogs. In the United States, approximately 7.5 million dogs enter shelters every year. As a result, 60% are euthanized.

Why does this problem exist? The two main root causes are:

- Irresponsible and accidental breeding
- Owners who fail to integrate the dog into the home, which results in relinquishment

Why People Surrender Dogs

The following are major excuses owners give when they relinquish their dog. They generally come under the category of lack of commitment or failure to train. They are listed here to show that all dogs in shelters are not bad dogs. They are victims of circumstance and uninformed owners. With patience and care they can make good family pets.

1. Landlord objects/Moving

Like a lot of problems in the world today, a few irresponsible people have ruined the freedoms of the responsible. Property managers usually object because of bitter past experiences with irresponsible owners. These dog owners let their dogs bark, chew, destroy landscaping and act without any consideration for their neighbors. The root cause in this case, and in most cases, stems from behavior problems. Dogs are not successfully trained and instructed in what is, and what is not acceptable. Owners don't know how to communicate and have failed to establish their leadership role with their dog. You can be successful adopting a dog relinquished for this reason if you:

- Obtain permission for the dog in writing before you obtain him.
- Understand dog behavior and positive reinforcement.
- Train your dog in basic home obedience or retain the services of a reputable behaviorist (ask a vet).

- Offer your landlord a pet security deposit.
- Have references ready that mention your pet.
- Practice responsible dog ownership (i.e.: license, identify, spay/neuter, immediately pick up waste, vaccinations, obedience school)
- Encourage the landlord to meet your well-groomed and well-behaved dog.
- Show a willingness to have the landlord visit.
- Make it clear that you will promptly clean up any mess left by the pet.
- Don't be discouraged if an ad says *no pets;* some landlords are flexible and make concessions for well-behaved dogs.

Photo by Sumner Fowler, Marin Humane Society

2. Not enough time for the dog

Work schedules change, kids lose interest, adults are tired after a hard day's work and the dog is left to himself in the back yard or garage. The owners have a hard time understanding why their dog barks so much, digs in the yard or escapes to wander the neighborhood. When they do pay attention, the dog is so excited to see them he jumps up, is hard to control and in general, acts like a dingbat. If the dog could communicate in English, he would say: "Let me be with you, tell me how I can please you. I am a social, pack animal and I need your company."

According to an American Animal Hospital Survey in 1994, 75% of dog owners spend at least 45 minutes to more than one hour each day engaged in activities with their pets, and 69% of dog owners give their pets as much attention as they would their children. It is not uncommon for owners to feel guilty. In fact, 76% occasionally or frequently felt guilt for not spending enough time with or giving enough attention to their pet. Ideally, dogs do best if they can function in an environment where they perceive an activity or purpose.

Before you obtain a dog, make sure you have enough quality time to spend with the dog. This is a very popular reason for surrender. You can deal successfully with a dog that was relinquished for this reason by:

- Scheduling time for exercise, training and play with your dog, especially in the morning.
- Prioritizing your time to include your best friend.
- Asking a dependable neighborhood boy or girl if they would like to play and walk your dog during the day.
- Using the services of a pet sitter or doggy day care center.
- Integrating the dog inside the home with the family.
- Learn how to show your dog the rules of the house.

3. Owner dies

Photo by Click, the Photo Connection

Perhaps the most tragic reason for relinquishment is the death of the owner. These dogs usually gave comfort and companionship to their owners when their health was failing. Unfortunately, no arrangements were made and there is no one to care for them. Most of these dogs are easy to take into your home. They are usually mature dogs that know house rules. It may take time for the dog to adjust, but soon, with patience and care, they will come to accept their new family.

- Make sure your pet is provided for in your will.

4. Cost

There are some people who get a dog and have not considered the expense involved. It costs a minimum of $300 per year to care for a dog. Costs include adoption fees, veterinary care and vaccines, training, boarding, registration fees, food, grooming supplies, toys and equipment. Adoption fees are charged to offset the costs involved with providing shelter, food, shots, and a license plus any spay/neuter surgery, identification or other related expense. A Gallup poll "Pet Census" revealed the average owners spend $1,500 per year on their pets. The yearly cost of feeding is estimated by multiplying the weight of the dog times $4. The biggest costs will be the first and last years of the dog's life.

- Make sure your budget includes proper care for your pet.

5. Lost interest

The little cuddly puppy that was so cute is now a 100-pound force. The dog that played a tough game of tug-of-war is too rough. When people purchase a dog they have a vision of the perfect dog they would like to have. Usually, this is the dog of their youth, or the perfect neighbor dog, or the dog they saw in the movies or on television. They are disappointed when their dog doesn't live up to expectations, when the Golden Retriever is hyper or the Shetland Sheepdog barks. When there is a gap between the expected behavior and the behavior exhibited, there is disappointment. Disappointment turns to neglect and neglect to relinquishment.

The main cause of disappointment is unexpected behavior problems that go unresolved. What people don't understand is that the dog is looking for direction from the master(s). When communication is lacking, dogs revert to natural tendencies that may not be acceptable in the human world in which they live. Sometimes dogs exhibit negative behaviors just to receive attention. You can avoid this situation by:

- Knowing BEFORE you get a dog the responsibilities of dog ownership. Do you truly have the desire and the commitment for a canine companion?

- Taking an obedience class. A successful relationship starts with an early obedience class that teaches a thorough understanding of a dog's nature and its needs.
- Keeping the dog indoors and making the dog a part of the family.
- Giving the relationship a chance to develop and being confident that inappropriate behavior will be corrected.
- Knowing that dogs will not be perfect and, like children, have their own personality.
- Investing time and care to achieve a well-mannered, responsive canine companion.

If you are able to adopt a dog that was relinquished because the owner lost interest, you can be the recipient of a dog that is loyal and eager to please.

6. Divorce

This unfortunate situation results in the dissolution of the home and the division of possessions. The dog is sent to the shelter because the divorced parties find they lack the ability to care for the dog. These dogs make wonderful pets to adopt but they have probably been on an emotional roller coaster.

- Give the dog time to adjust to your home.
- Don't yell or raise your voice.

Photo by Click, the Photo Connection

7. Had a new baby

Some families neglect their dog when they are faced with the demands of a new child. What often happens is the dog loses quality time and attention in favor of the new baby. The dog that resided inside is relegated to the back yard or garage. The dog resorts to negative behaviors in order to get attention from its owners. You can deal successfully with a dog and a baby by:

- Allocating quality time with the dog.
- Including the dog in social gatherings.
- Making sure the first meeting is positive.
- Choosing a breed that has a history of getting along with young children.

See Introducing Your Dog to a New Infant.

8. Fleas

Sometimes owners relinquish their dogs because of simple grooming and maintenance problems. Every owner needs to have a thorough understanding of how to rid their pets and house of fleas. This is a simple problem to solve.

- If you can't cope with flea problems, don't get a dog.

See How to Deal Successfully With Fleas.

9. The dog is too dumb

There is an old saying, "There is no such thing as a bad dog, only uninformed owners." If owners give up a dog for this reason, they probably don't have a clue about dogs. Some dogs might take more persistence, but every dog can be trained using positive reinforcement methods. Some people use force techniques with varying intensity. In the long run this does not work. The dog loses motivation. The owners blame the dog when, in fact, it's the owners' own lack of education.

- A kind, considerate owner that takes a basic obedience class will be successful with a dog relinquished for this reason.
- Use positive reinforcement; it motivates.

10. Unsuitability

This usually occurs when the family members did not sit down and discuss the joint responsibility of dog ownership. They did not take the time to do the research and understand a dog's characteristics and needs and its compatibility with their life style. Usually the dog was obtained on an impulse. Sometimes it was bought as a present. The cute little puppy was irresistible. They did not know the long coat would require constant brushing and grooming or the big, strong dog that the husband chose would be in the care of his wife, who could not deal effectively with the dog. Their loss can be your treasure.

- Practice good basic dog training and care to achieve a successful relationship.

11. Ill treatment

This is the saddest category of relinquished dogs because these dogs have been abused, neglected and treated cruelly through no fault of their own. They had the misfortune of being subjected to ignorant owners who are mentally unbalanced. Cases include dogs that are tied up and left to starve, dogs that are deliberately burned, dogs that are kept in tight, crowded cages and dogs that are used for fighting.

The list of barbaric horrors goes on and on. Shelters care for these dogs and nurse them back to health whenever possible. Sadly, many of these dogs must be put down. When shelter personnel place these dogs up for adoption, the dogs are evaluated for temperament problems. If any exist, the dogs are destroyed. You can be successful in adopting an abused dog if:

- You look at a long-term rehabilitation program consisting of love, gentle care and plenty of patience.
- You understand these dogs need to have their confidence rebuilt through positive reinforcement, using lots of praise, happy talk, play and treats.
- You do not punish negative behavior or use threatening body language.
- You prevent negative behavior from occurring.

12. Impulse buying and impulse accepting

A large number of people obtain their dogs on impulse. They give puppies to unsuspecting recipients for holidays and birthdays. They walk by the pet store in the mall and see a cute little fluffy dog they just have to have. They answer an ad in the newspaper. Got to have one. They visit a friend's house, and the friend introduces her accidental litter. Soon the adorable puppy is romping in a new home. This is called impulse accepting. Statistics show a large number of impulse dogs in the shelter after one year: "It just didn't work." You can avoid this:

- Know what you're getting yourself into. Do your homework. Make the selection of a dog a rational, well-thought-out decision.

13. Surrender of a litter

People relinquish litters that are the direct result of irresponsible matings. Owners cannot care or find homes for these puppies so they "dump" them at the shelter. They are usually the result of careless, accidental breeding by dogs who were not spayed and neutered. This is the primary cause of pet overpopulation and why advocates work so hard to inform people about the need to spay/neuter.

Stray Dogs and the Cycle of Broken Bonds

Fifty-six percent of the dogs in shelters across the United States come in as strays. These dogs are listed as strays because they are not wearing identification. If they were, authorities could return the dogs to their homes. Many owners have abandoned their dogs to wander the streets, hoping they will find a home.

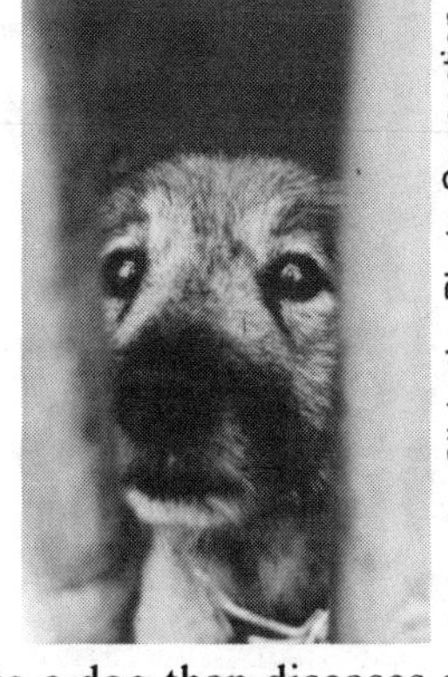

Photo by Click, the Photo Connection

What went wrong? How did the bond of mutual friendship fail? Unresolved behavior problems are more lethal to a dog than diseases and accidents combined. When owners make no effort to train or their efforts are unsuccessful, it sets off a sequence of events that are often fatal to the dog. Owners become frustrated after failed attempts at changing the dog's bad habits and begin to lose interest. The dog is relegated to the back yard, where it is generally bored and neglected. This makes the situation worse. After all, the dog is a social animal. The dog starts barking, chewing and exhibiting other signals and signs of distress and boredom. Often the roaming instinct is triggered; other times the owners don't bother to contain them. Most of these dogs don't have identification. Sooner or later they are caught by an animal-control officer or they are brought to shelters by a citizen, many of the dogs in a state of severe neglect. Once impounded, they have a slim chance of survival — especially if they are large and over the age of two.

Euthanasia: A Dignified Death

Euthanasia comes from the Greek words: *eu,* which means "easy" and *thanatos,* which means "death." Thus, euthanasia means to use the least painful and most dignified means of death for reasons of mercy.

The simple fact is that the number of animals brought into shelters far exceeds their capacity and resources. Unfortunately, it is necessary to humanely take pet lives. Shelter personnel are left with the regretful task of making life and death decisions, for to abandon these creatures would result in a far worse fate. Often these decisions are based on age, injury, sickness, or problems of temperament. Sadly, when space dictates, good tempered, young, healthy dogs are euthanized.

What You Can Do to Solve Pet Overpopulation

1. Spay/neuter your pet at an early age, well before sexual maturity (6 months). Encourage others to do the same.
2. Don't be an uneducated owner. Most dog owners experience problems. Have the knowledge and confidence to work out any problem. Take a basic dog obedience class and learn about basic dog behavior.
3. Safeguard your pet. Don't let your dog roam.
4. Make sure identification is in place and secured with an O ring. Identification and license tags are the main ways dogs are reunited with their owners.
5. Adopt a dog from an animal shelter or reputable rescue.

6. If you never have bred before and you have the slightest inclination to breed your dog, don't. Leave breeding to knowledgeable, experienced professional breeders who are dedicated to improving the health and temperament of the breed, have quality breeding stock, guarantee their dogs and have established an excellent reputation. A litter will contribute to the canine overpopulation crisis. Too many stray and unwanted dogs are the product of a casual breeding or an accidental breeding. When a dog is born from an unplanned litter, chances are it will be condemned to a life of misery, deprivation and death.
7. Support your local nonprofit humane society, shelter and low-cost spay/neuter organization with financial donations or by volunteering your services.
8. Take responsibility for your pet. If, for whatever reason, you need to give up your dog, make every effort to find a good home. Check with your friends and neighbors. Don't kid yourself into thinking someone will come to the shelter and give your dog a home on their farm. Statistics tell us that approximately 60% of all dogs that enter shelters will be euthanized. If your dog is over the age of two, it will have a very slim chance of being rehomed. Don't place an ad that says, "Free to good home." Many of those dogs end up in research labs, in the hands of brokers or someone who is not committed to the responsibilities of dog ownership.
9. If your dog is experiencing behavior problems, get the help of a trained professional. Call your veterinarian or pet store and ask for a referral to a good behaviorist or trainer. Many problems are unknowingly caused by owner handling errors.
10. If you are going to move, take your pet with you. Talk to your future landlord and explain that you have a well-behaved dog. Take and pass a basic obedience class and, or, AKC Good Citizenship Test and show the certificate to your landlord. Offer to make a dog security deposit that will protect the owner from financial loss to his or her property. Don't sign a lease until you know the property accepts dogs.

Don't be part of the problem. • Be part of the solution!

Photo by David Jensen, Alaska Pet-ography

Statistics prove that two of these adorable puppies will be relinquished before they are one year of age.

The Importance of Spay / Neuter

Spay/neuter is the single most important thing you can do to fight pet overpopulation. Approximately 75% of dogs in shelters are mixed breeds. They are a result of owners who carelessly refuse to have their dogs spayed or neutered.

Over 4 million healthy, friendly dogs will be euthanized in the United States this year simply because there are not enough good homes. In the male, neutering will reduce territorial fighting and roaming instincts (80% of the dogs killed on the highways are unaltered males looking to mate). In the female, spaying will benefit you by eliminating blood spotting during the heat period, pregnancy complications and tumors of the ovaries, uterus, breast and vagina.

To prevent unwanted pregnancies, *make this decision at an early age* (well before the first heat cycle in female dogs, as early as eight weeks for males and females). Spaying or neutering is the removal of the reproductive organs and is considered major surgery. Your pet will be given a sedative, a general anesthetic and will be unconscious. There is some minimal risk involved just as there is with any surgery and anesthesia, but a skilled veterinarian keeps the risks minimal. Your dog will feel no pain during the operation. There may be some minor discomfort for a day or so after the surgery. Your pet may be able to go home within twenty-four hours of the surgery. Consult with your veterinarian.

The Humane Society of the United States, The American Kennel Club, The American Humane Association, The American Veterinary Medical Association endorse early-age (8-16 weeks) spay/neutering.

Spay / Neuter Facts vs. Myths

Myth I'll have a litter and make a few bucks.

Fact The income of having a litter does not equal the expenses incurred, such as stud fees, food, veterinarian bills, advertising, health certifications and shots, not to mention all the time and effort to ensure health of the mother and litter during two months of pregnancy and two months of nursing. If complications develop such as Cesarean birth or if any puppies have medical problems, you could be looking at a huge loss.

Myth My animal will be deprived of reproduction.

Fact There is no physical or behavioral benefit for a dog to bear or sire a litter. Pets want and need affection, warmth, food, shelter and companionship — not parenthood.

Myth Neutering will change my pet's personality.

Fact You will benefit by any personality change. Neutered pets tend to be calmer, more contented animals. Males are less likely to engage in several undesirable behaviors including mounting, urine marking in the house, roaming and aggression toward other male dogs.

Myth Neutering my pet will make it fat and lazy.

Fact Too much food and too little exercise lead to obesity.

Myth We will just safeguard our bitch when she is in heat.

Fact This is not an easy task. The desire to be mounted is strong. It only takes a moment and it's done. Most owners never knew it happened until they see their dog is pregnant or about to give birth.

Myth I want to teach my children about birth.

Fact There are many ways to teach children about the reproductive process that do not result in the birth of unwanted animals. In reality, what parents teach is irresponsibility and a low value for life.

Chances are most of these puppies will be condemned to a life of misery, abuse and death.

Myth I'll find good homes for my litter.

Fact Most people are inexperienced with placing puppies in good homes and end up "getting rid of" the pups. Friends who say they want a puppy start groping for excuses when the time comes to place them. When dogs have puppies, each of the puppies is capable of producing their own litter, thereby compounding the overpopulation problem. Even if you do find homes for the litter, you will still be contributing to the overpopulation crisis by taking the homes of other dogs whose births were less preventable. You must also be prepared to take these dogs back if any problems arise throughout their life. And, remember, only one in five dogs stay in their first home.

2

Selecting a Shelter Dog

Advantages and Disadvantages of Shelter Adoptions

Advantages

When you visit a shelter you will find dogs of all ages, sizes, shapes and colors; mixed breed and purebreds.

- The initial cost of purchase is less expensive and usually includes shots, license and possibly spay/neuter surgery.
- Most dogs from shelters respond very well, with time, to loving care and attention. They relish your company.
- An adult dog is mature in appearance.
- Some experts say mixed-breed dogs are more even-tempered and less prone to medical problems.
- Shelter dogs are usually spayed/neutered or arrangements are made to provide this at a low cost. The animal is checked for health problems.
- An adult dog is probably housebroken and may have had some obedience training.
- You don't have the hassles of puppyhood and the frustration of the adolescent stage.
- You would be saving a dog's life.

Disadvantages

Sometimes you don't know what experiences the dog has had and how it affected its temperament.

- Sometimes the need for your presence is so strong, the new dog can become anxious when left alone.
- It will take from one to twelve weeks for the dog to acclimate to your home. You must be patient and attentive during this time.

Dogs' Best Friends — People Who Rescue and Rehome

Photo by Click, the Photo Connection

There are a variety of people and organizations dedicated to saving the lives of unwanted dogs. These people fight a constant battle to find good, lasting homes for dogs, often with limited resources and funding.

The majority of these people are caring, knowledgeable and compassionate. They are faced with numerous challenges and pressures driven by the need to find suitable adopters for unwanted dogs before their time runs out. Society owes them a debt of gratitude. They are the ones who live close to the tragedy and see the needless waste of these wonderful creatures. They are painfully aware of how many times humans have abandoned their dogs and failed to live up to their responsibilities.

The satisfaction for people who work in rescue is placing dogs in good, permanent homes. They can take comfort in knowing their efforts have saved an animal from needless death and have provided a family with the joys of canine companionship.

Animal Welfare and Adoption Organizations

There are a large number of shelter agencies, groups and individuals that respond to the needs of dogs in their community. They vary in size and structure from large, public institutions with huge budget requirements to small kennels run by one or two dog lovers who provide foster care in their home.

Most of the institutions function according to their funding. The better the funding, the more services they can provide. In this day of perennial budget deficits, shelter administrators are challenged to provide an effective animal care and control program while constantly faced with shrinking budgets. Grass-roots workers who are involved in rescue often use their own resources to rehome dogs.

Public shelter funding comes primarily from tax dollars. Funds are allocated due to the importance local officials place on animal care and control. Private shelters function based on the generosity of donors and the small fee charged for the adoption. According to the Humane Society of the United States, an adequately-funded animal control program should be budgeted at three to five dollars per citizen.

National Advocates:

Humane Society of the United States

The Humane Society of the United States is a nonprofit organization dedicated to humane treatment of animals through educational, legislative, investigative and legal means. Founded in 1954, the HSUS and its ten regional offices work to foster respect, understanding and compassion for all living creatures. HSUS is not affiliated with, nor a governing agency for local shelters. The term "humane society" is generic.

American Humane Association

Founded in 1877, AHA is a nonprofit organization dedicated to the prevention of cruelty, neglect, abuse, and exploitation of children and animals. Their mission is to assure that the interests and well-being of children and animals are fully, effectively, and humanely guaranteed by an aware and caring society. The American Humane Association is not affiliated with, nor a governing agency for local shelters.

American Society for the Prevention of Cruelty to Animals

American Society for the Prevention of Cruelty to Animals (ASPCA) is both a local shelter for New York City and headquarters for national educational programs. The society was founded in 1866 by Henry Bergh and modeled after England's Royal Society for the Prevention of Cruelty to Animals (RSPCA). The ASPCA has taken care of needy animals in the city of New York for over 129 years. Its mission is to attack indifference and inhumanity toward animals through education. ASPCA is not affiliated with, nor a governing agency for local shelters. The term "Society for the Prevention of Cruelty to Animals (SPCA)" is generic and can be used by any group.

Public Organizations:

City and County Animal Control

Photo by Click, the Photo Connection

For the sake of public health and safety and the quality of life in the community, it is imperative that local governments provide animal control services. These agencies are set up to manage animal-related complaints and problems. Responsibilities include the operation of community shelters that provide temporary food and refuge for orphaned dogs, cats and other domestic animals until they can be adopted or claimed by their owner, enforcement of animal control ordinances, pick up and receiving of strays, responding to animals that bite and are vicious, and investigating animal neglect and cruelty cases. Many agencies provide access to affordable sterilization services. Agencies receive owner relinquished dogs and rehome them if possible. If no homes can be found and the kennel space is near capacity they are left with no alternative but to humanely euthanize unwanted dogs.

Most state laws require stray dogs to be held for a minimum number of days before they can be destroyed. City and county animal control shelters are usually funded with tax dollars. Areas of responsibility can be divided by city and county jurisdictions. Many counties and some cities privatize their animal control operation by contracting out those services to humane societies and SPCAs. Check with your local police department if you are uncertain who performs animal control in your community.

Private Organizations:

Humane Societies

These private, nonprofit, independent organizations provide shelter and adoptions for relinquished animals and investigate reports of cruelty, abuse and neglect. Additional services depend on the generosity of the community and the caring volunteers needed to staff them. Some are able to offer spay/neuter surgery at reduced rates or free, behavioral counseling, lost and found hot lines, educational programs, pet-assisted therapy programs, senior citizen free adoptions and rental referrals to landlords who accept pets. In some communities, humane societies receive contracts to perform animal control, which makes them responsible for law enforcement and providing shelter for stray pets. Some humane societies accept owner relinquished dogs only on a space available basis. Some do not take in strays. Generally, humane societies are more selective than government run animal control agencies in the screening process of potential adopters. All shelter adoption efforts focus on finding mutually compatible homes. Local humane societies are not nationally affiliated or controlled. They function independently with their own board of directors, bylaws and policies. They always require charitable contributions from the community to survive.

SPCA

SPCA has became a generic name that is used by many shelters across the country. There are no membership rules, control or affiliation with the ASPCA. Each agency is free to establish policies and procedures as it sees fit. SPCAs are nonprofit and function with the same purpose as humane societies. Each shelter is responsible for raising funds, primarily through charitable donations to meet their operating expenses.

Shelter Support Groups and Volunteers

Dedicated volunteers work to assist community shelters with fundraising, staffing and maintaining the kennels. Their work includes help with adoptions, walking and playing with the dogs, lost and found and spay/neutering educational programs. The effectiveness of shelter programs can be largely determined by the efforts of these hard-working, caring and selfless individuals.

Choosing and Caring for a Shelter Dog

Breed Rescue

Thousands of people donate their time, energy and resources to save abandoned or mistreated purebred dogs from bad situations that could cost them their life. Mostly they are composed of breeders and dog owners who have developed a deep fondness for a specific breed. The vast majority are caring, ethical individuals who work for no financial gain. Many represent breed specialty clubs, while others work independently.

Breed rescue individuals work to develop a relationship of mutual trust with the shelters, screen potential adopters, compile waiting lists of people who are suitable for adoption, charge a sum necessary to recover costs and release dogs only after they have been spayed / neutered. Some foster dogs in their home while others act as a referral and direct inquiries to shelters or individuals where the dogs are available.

Greyhound Rescue

The average greyhound dog's life can last well over twelve years. Their racing life can last four to six years — if they run fast. If they don't, they are callously destroyed. Racetrack breeders breed constantly in hopes of getting a dog that is a consistent winner, destroying the ones that don't measure up. Several Greyhound Rescue groups have stepped in to save these gentle dogs and prevent their slaughter. They have lobbied legislatures to enact laws, and they have put pressure on racing associations to stop this practice. Greyhound Pets of America, founded by Darren Riggs, works to save racing greyhounds by placing them in suitable homes. You can reach them by calling 1-800-366-1472 or call the National Greyhound Association at 1-800-GHOUNDS.

Independent Organizations

These groups are dedicated to rescue and rehome both mixed breed and purebred dogs. Some are able to offer temporary foster care, while others are able to act as a referral to find suitable homes for needy dogs.

Photo by Sumner Fowler, Marin Humane Society

The Second-Chance Dog

There are many wonderful dogs that people have forsaken just waiting for a chance at a new home. Anyone who knows dogs and has been to a shelter is amazed at the quality of dogs represented. A common response by adopters is, "I can't believe this fine dog was abandoned and available for adoption." Shelter personnel have received thousands and thousands of letters from adopters who have expressed their enjoyment and their appreciation for connecting them with their adopted dog. These relationships work. But they are not without effort. Future adopters must be aware of common misconceptions when viewing dogs in a shelter.

People commonly believe that what you see is what you get. This is not necessarily true. Most dogs are under stress from the kennel experience. By nature, dogs are sentient, social animals. When they are abandoned they have a hard time coping with the emotional ordeal of their situation. When you visit the kennel you will find some of the dogs sitting quietly, staring out at the world. They are confined and lonely, surrounded by strange noises and people. Some may shiver and shake simply because they are not familiar with being anywhere except in a home. Others react differently. Many dogs exhibit minor behavior problems. It is common for them to bark and be out of sorts. Usually, these are minor problems that can be easily modified over time. The trick is to look not so much at what the dog is, but at what it will become under the guidance of a kind, knowledgeable owner.

Many people think you can't train adult dogs. Not so. *You can train an adult dog.* Shelter dogs need patience, understanding and consistent leadership. They need you to teach them how to act. Once they know how to act, they will become more secure and confident. They need owners who are patient and who will take the time to work with them. They will become the dog you envision, but it will not happen overnight.

Most of these dogs are the consequence of owners who did not make the time nor have the understanding to deal successfully with their needs. When you take on the responsibility of a shelter dog, you will have the satisfaction of knowing your efforts can make the difference in saving a dog's life.

Selection Criteria:

Size

If you are planning to adopt a dog from the shelter, you want to consider size. Your living space should be suitable for the size of the dog. Generally, smaller dogs are more accepted in society. Rental units and condos are more apt to accept dogs under a certain height and weight. Smaller dogs are less costly to feed, and they require less exercise. The terrier breeds were used to hunt small rodents and foxes. They had to stand up to anything. These traits can translate into a dog that is feisty, smart and active. Larger dogs have been bred for hunting, herding and guarding and can provide a reassuring presence. They generally require more space and exercise. They are more expensive to feed.

Coat

Consider the amount of care the adult coat will require. Every dog needs regular grooming. Some dogs require more grooming time due to the nature of their coat. Dogs such as the Collie, Maltese, Cockers, Lhasa Apso, Shih Tzu, St. Bernard, and Old English Sheepdog require extensive time combing out knots and tangles and caring for their coat. A large number of dogs shed. For most dogs this happens twice yearly. For some, like the Dalmatian, it is constant. Another factor pertaining to a dog's coat is flea treatment. It is easier to treat fleas in short-haired dogs. Consider the amount of time you are willing to spend tending to your dog's grooming needs. Can you afford the service of a professional groomer?

Purebred or Mixed Breed

Photo by Click, the Photo Connection

Purebred dogs comprise approximately 25% of shelter dogs. They are genetically more predictable due to centuries of selective breeding. Dogs were bred to perform certain tasks, which help serve the needs of the community. Today many of these tasks are obsolete but the dogs still retain their instincts and general appearance. When mature they should conform to the "breed standard" for physical characteristics and temperament. You will not be able to register or participate in conformation shows with a purebred dog obtained from a shelter. They are exclusively pet dogs.

If you decide you want a purebred dog, first check with your local shelters. If the breed you seek is not available, seek the service of a purebred rescue group in your area. They will place your name on a waiting list. When a dog becomes available, they will notify you. Call the American Kennel Club at 212/696-8200 or Project Breed at 202/244-0065 and ask for the rescue contact for the national breed club or local specialty club of the dog you prefer. But remember, rescue groups spay / neuter and withhold papers. You will not be able to breed these dogs.

Mixed-breed or mongrel dogs are combinations of other breeds and are usually the result of unplanned pregnancies. They comprise approximately 75% of shelter dogs. Generally mixed breed dogs are healthier, more even tempered and make excellent companion dogs.

Photo by Sumner Fowler, Marin Humane Society

Male or Female

After you spay or neuter your dog the sex is of little importance. The female dogs are usually a shade smaller than male dogs. Females may have a gentler nature. Unspayed females go into heat twice a year, resulting in blood spotting for several days. You need to be patient on walks with a male because male dogs want and need to mark their territory. They do this by lifting their leg and squirting scented urine. Unaltered males will become more agitated when local bitches come into season. If you have another dog, be aware of compatible combinations. For the first-time dog owner, the sex of the dog is personal preference.

Puppy or Adult Dog

Puppies are preferred by the majority of the people, but adult dogs have a lot to offer. It is very satisfying for a lot of people to watch a puppy grow and to influence the pup's development. Puppies take a lot of hard work, patience and training. Puppies require almost constant attention. You can never be certain how the pup will turn out. Many people say it is like raising kids.

Adult dogs, on the other hand, are mature. The size and coat will be immediately evident. The adult dog may already be trained to understand walking on a leash, where to go to relieve himself and obedience commands. His personality and activity level is formed, so you may be able to match those traits with your life style. Contrary to the old myth, adult dogs are very trainable. They require a lot more patience, sensitivity and understanding. Some may have negative experiences that will take time to modify.

Do You Want a Guard Dog or Watch Dog?

Most breeds are territorial and will naturally alert their owners to the presence of an intruder. Selective breeding has produced a few breeds that are genetically programmed to guard and in some cases attack an intruder. All breeds can be trained to be watchdogs. However, if you are looking for a dog that intimidates or attacks, you must consider that you are arousing aggressive tendencies in your dog. In order to properly control your dog you will need professional guard dog training.

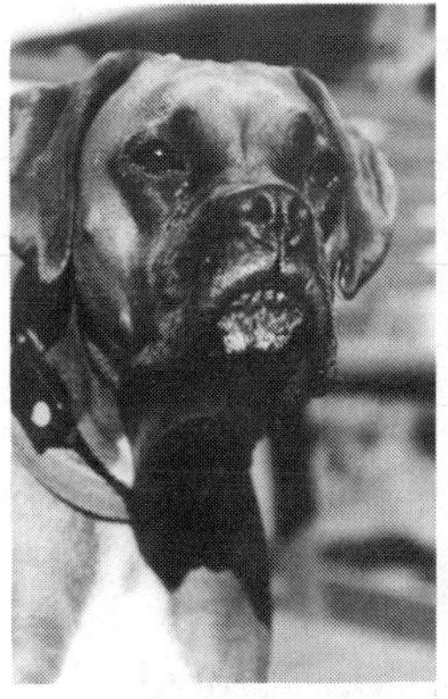
Photo by Click, the Photo Connection

This is expensive. Guard dogs or attack dogs must be very carefully trained and receive continual retraining. They need to know how, where and when to bite. Professional police dogs cost thousands of dollars and train weekly. If you think you can have a guard dog and not train him, the result will probably be a dog that is confused around strangers, a dog that will bark and growl indiscriminately at anyone, including your family. You should also be aware of the liability. If anyone is bitten while acting lawfully, you could be responsible for damages. Your dog would be confiscated and destroyed if judged a threat to the public. Additional punitive costs could be awarded if you were found to be harboring a vicious dog.

For people who are concerned about intruders, a watchdog is a big asset. A watchdog will only bark to alert its owner that a stranger is on the premises. It will not attack. Studies have indicated most intruders are less apt to burglarize a house with a barking dog. Every dog has the potential to be trained as a watchdog. Watchdogs can range in degrees of alertness from very alert dogs that bark at the slightest provocation to dogs that bark when they are confronted by a stranger on the premises. A few dogs are so friendly they will not bark at all.

A guard dog is very protective of its territory and possesses instincts to hold intruders at bay by aggressively barking and growling and, or attacking. The more popular guard dogs are the Rottweiler, German Shepherd, Doberman, Staffordshire Bull Terrier, Akita and Chow Chow. They are also among the top breeds relinquished and destroyed because owners were unable to control aggressive tendencies that were unwittingly provoked.

Sound Temperament

Responsible shelters evaluate incoming dogs for the soundness of their temperament. Temperament is basically a dog's personality that is influenced by its genetics, its environment, its early socialization during its imprint period and its owner's handling. A sound dog has a stable, well-balanced mental make-up. They are confident when faced with various stimuli. They are not overly threatened or disturbed. Generally, those dogs displaying unsound temperaments are euthanized.

Most dogs in shelters will exhibit some signs of stress due to the nature of their situations. Dogs handle stress differently. Some will show shyness and some may be outright depressed. Barking is quite common in shelters. Most dogs love attention and, because they are deprived, will bark to get noticed. Don't be overly concerned about barking in a kennel situation. If a dog shows its teeth, growls or lunges aggressively at the cage, don't pursue it. Call it to the attention of shelter management.

The Adoption Process

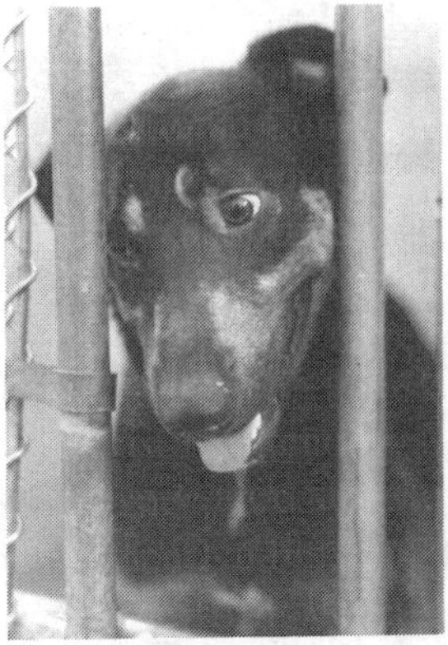

Dedicated personnel in adoption agencies work hard to place pets in permanent homes. Every effort is made to ensure that each pet offered for adoption is the kind of pet you would want for your family and one that will fit well in your home. Dogs that have apparent health or behavior problems are not put up for adoption.

Photo by Sumner Fowler, Marin Humane Society

You may be asked to fill out a questionnaire at many shelters. This questionnaire will help to determine a good match. Most agencies require that you be 18 years old and that you have the consent of your landlord. The screening process is designed to protect dogs and future owners from regretful situations. Returned dogs are subjected to more stress, which makes future placement more difficult.

The dog is eligible for adoption after the state-designated hold period on strays, which can be from three to seven days. This allows time for owners to claim their lost pet without the dog being sent to a new home. It also gives shelters the time to do a thorough evaluation of the dog. Sometimes when the dog becomes available it is desired by more than one adopter. Shelters have different procedures for handling this. Some use first-come, some use a lottery and draw names out of a hat.

Many shelters will create a profile of the dog's behavior and any known pertinent facts. For instance a card might read, *not good with small children,* or *not a good dog for a standard working home, dominant, housetrained, obedience trained,* etc.

Adoptions usually include spay or neuter (or a commitment to have it done), vaccinations and health examinations. You may be required to show verification that the pet is allowed at your residence, proof of residence, and you might be asked to introduce your other family dog to make sure they can get along. Fees are usually under $75. Call your local agency for their fees and requirements.

Choosing and Caring for a Shelter Dog

Observing Dogs in Shelters

Safety is always the number one concern. Chances are nothing will happen but it's better to be safe than sorry. Potential injury can be averted by recognizing the dogs body posture and facial expression. When walking through a kennel, use a non-threatening, casual manner. Maintain a confident posture while using a friendly tone of voice that is neither threatening nor submissive. Try to greet a dog on one knee without staring into it's eyes. Please observe the following cautions:

Never stare in the eyes of a kennel dog.

Never hover over the dog and never use your hands from above.

Don't force or drag animals in or out of cages.

Never startle a sleeping dog.

Never make loud, sudden noises.

Don't corner a dog.

Do not hold any animal to your face.

Don't try to break up a dog fight.

Never take food or other objects from an unknown dog.

Never place an unknown dog in a subordinate position.

Always use a lead (leash) when handling a dog.

Chaperone children and make sure they don't abuse a dog

Evaluating Dogs in Kennels

Imagine being taken from your home and placed in confinement with others. Would you be stressed? Would you be yourself? Would you recover if you were placed in a loving, supportive environment? The vast majority of dogs in shelters are good dogs. They need consideration and a period of readjustment. There is no foolproof method to evaluate the temperament of a shelter dog Although there are no definitive tests, you can get a "feel" for the dog by performing a few exercises.

Evaluation Exercises that give you a general feel for the dog:

Training	Command the dog to "Sit." Push his rear end down. If the dog does not obey, don't persist. Praise if he complies.
Play Drive	In a safe area use a tennis ball or other desirable object and interact with the dog.
Dominance	Dog stands stiff, eyes will stare, ears erect, tail will be held straight-up and curve over the back, hackles or hair on back stands up.
Affection	Touch and interact with the dog.
Harsh Treatment	Observe the dog when you swing your hands over it's head. Does it cower?
Energy Level	Most dogs will be happy to have your attention. They will enjoy the activity and show it. Their energy level should subside when they adjust to your home.
On a Leash	Does the dog walk without pulling? Is it friendly towards other people or animals.
Handling	Does the dog allow you to touch it's face or collar? Can you touch it's body?

Health Examination

Negative Signs

Overall	Sluggishness, weakness, or reluctance to move
Eyes	Redness, cloudiness, squinting or discharge
Nose	Sores, thick mucus or crusty discharge
Ears	Discharge, sores scratching or foul smell
Mouth	Excessive drooling, abnormal panting or bleeding gums
Skin	Wounds and sores, rashes, balding areas, fleas
Lameness	Limping, holding up of paw, reluctance to walk or cries of pain

Choosing and Caring for a Shelter Dog

Questions You Need to Have Answered at the Shelter

1. Check out the dog's history. Why is it up for adoption? If no history is available and the dog is affectionate toward you, don't worry too much about why it's there.
2. Is it friendly toward children? Some breeds and breed mixes can accept and tolerate toddlers, some accept mature children, and some don't care for any kids at all.
3. Has it ever bitten anyone? Aggression is very difficult to deal with even for experienced owners (if it is firmly established). Sometimes there are circumstances in which a dog was agitated and provoked.
4. Is the dog housebroken? At first, all shelter dogs should be treated as if they were never house trained.
5. Was it an inside or outside dog?
6. What is the dog's physical condition? Is the dog's coat shiny and healthy? Are the teeth white and gums pink and firm? Is the weight right? Most veterinarians offer FREE exams for rescued animals. Does it require any special care?
7. Does it respond to obedience commands?
8. Is it shy or fearful? Is it active? Although a bouncy active dog may catch your eye, a quiet or reserved dog might be easier to live with and care for.
9. What is the dog's body posture saying? Is the tail tucked between its legs? Does it cower when your hand is raised above its head to pet it? Is it shy? Does it bark aggressively, growl or raise its hackles around you or other dogs? A family with children better heed these signs. These dogs may be better suited for an experienced owner who knows how to work to modify this temperament.
10. How does the pet react to play? Try to spend 30 minutes with your favorite. Many shelters have quiet areas where you can get to know the pet better. Take a ball and some treats and see how the dog responds to you and your family. Does it like to be touched? Don't be surprised if the dog is frisky, jumps up on you or pulls on the leash. Dogs act out of character in kennel situations. They will probably be excited from being out of the kennel and with people.
11. Does the dog mix well with other dogs or cats? The only way to test this is to bring your dog and see how they interact.

12. Is it used to riding in a car?
13. What is the dog being fed? Change to quality dog food if necessary. Change gradually. Dogs can develop soft stools from an abrupt change in the type of food they are fed.

Special Considerations for Puppies

Many of the considerations are the same in choosing a puppy as in selecting an adult dog. However, some puppies are usually separated from their mother before the normal time. Socialization (controlled positive exposure of a puppy to other people, other dogs, and objects) from six weeks to eighteen weeks is very important. Make sure they have up-to-date vaccines.

You should make sure you know the mature size, weight, coat and temperament of the dog. Consult a book on breed characteristics.

Try to determine the meekest and the most dominant puppies in the litter. Don't choose either if you are a first-time owner.

Visit the shelter during the week, when shelter personnel have more time. Ask them for their insights. Shelter workers and volunteers are concerned with creating the right match for permanent placements.

Pets for Seniors and Seniors for Pets

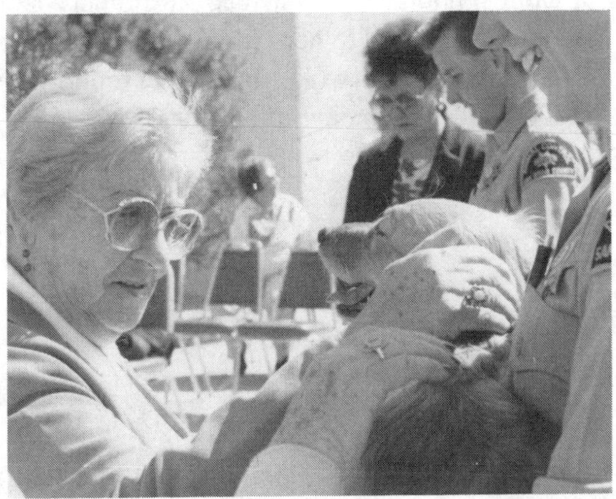

Seniors are living longer, they are more active and they are enjoying life in their retirement years. Many savvy seniors recognize the benefit of owning a dog. They realize the dog's amazing ability to comfort them when they are lonely, to guard them when they feel threatened and to provide a consistent source of loving companionship. Dogs encourage exercise and activity and can open up a whole new world for an older person. Studies have shown seniors are given a whole new lease on life when they have a dog to care for. Inquire at your local shelter or humane society about special senior adoption programs.

Laughter is the Best Medicine

Shelter work is emotionally and physically difficult. It is very frustrating to constantly experience humanity's failed animal relationships. The Santa Cruz SPCA has developed a healthy outlet for handling the frustrations that come with shelter work. When something amusing happens, employees record the experience in a log that is shared with fellow workers.

- James answered the phone yesterday, "Hello this is James. Can you help me?"
- Famous misspellings; "Shit Su," "*Flee* Collar," "arrested for *Salt* & Battery," "Larso Arso," "Dash Hound," "Rockwilder dog," "Sheet Su," "smells of *humane* urine," "Chiwawa," "left at *Male* box" (wonder how he could tell), "Dog had all his *Bordello* shots (where was he going?)," "Croker Spanial," "Bull massive," "Pep Bull,"
- A woman on the phone said she had a chocolate covered lab to bring in.
- A woman previously owned an Australian Cattle Dog in Utah. She said her dog loved to herd the cows and horses that grazed nearby. One morning she woke up to the sound of loud braying. She looked out the window to find her dog had herded a whole group of wild donkeys into her front yard and wouldn't let them leave.

3

Living with a Shelter Dog

Collect These Items Together Before Your Dog Arrives

1. A suitable bed or a thick lamb's wool pad.
2. An old blanket or a towel that is soft and easy to clean.
3. Two bowls, one for food and the other for water. Look for stoneware or stainless steel.
4. A nylon or leather buckle collar and leash. Never use a training collar (choker) until 5-6 months of age. If your dog is older than 6 months, you will need a training collar. Never keep it on the dog permanently. Use it only for training. Rolled leather collars are recommended for long-haired dogs.
5. Dog brush, comb, currycomb, dog shampoo, flea products and nail clippers.
6. Dog chews, like a good quality flat rawhide, sterilized large femur bone and a safe dog toy.
7. High-quality dog food formulated for the age of your new pet.
8. A good dog crate (it can be a big aid in training).

Naming Your Dog

Give your dog a fresh start with a new name. The first thing to remember is to use positive association when you say his new name. Grab some soft food treats. While standing alongside your dog say its new name in a pleased, happy voice. When the dog looks at you, give it a morsel of food. Repeat five times. The goal is to make the dog think good things are about to happen when it hears the sound of its name. Use a happy, high tone of voice.

Choosing and Caring for a Shelter Dog

According to a Gallup poll, some common names are Lady, Bear, Sam, Rusty, Scruffy, Shadow, Spike, Alex, Bandit, Brandy, Daisy, Dog, Fritz, Lucy and Molly. Avoid harsh sounding names like Thor. It can initiate a barking response. Never use the dog's name when you make a correction.

Identification

It is vitally important that you identify your dog immediately. Animal Control officials state one of the main causes of euthanizing is the fact dogs are turned in with no traceable identification. Any dog has the potential to get out and get lost. It is vitally important for your dog to wear a collar with his license number, and medallion with his name (some people include the word REWARD), your name, address and telephone number. Another method available is microchips. Microchips are becoming increasingly common nationwide, but your local shelters must be committed to using the scanner. Since there is more than one company marketing scanners and there is no standardization, it is important to check with your local shelters to determine the type of scanner they use before you select a supplier.

TIP: Don't use an S ring to hold dog tags. Use an O ring. S rings get caught, easily open and the ID gets lost.

Toys

The more toys the better. Fetch toys such as a tennis ball work great. Dogs respond well to lamb's wool chews of various shapes and sizes. Don't use an old pair of shoes. Dogs don't know the difference between old and new. Quality flat rawhide chews, Kongs™, Nylabones™ and sterilized large femur bones are favored by many dogs.

Dogproof Your Home

We want to PREVENT negative behaviors from occurring and we want to REINFORCE POSITIVE BEHAVIORS. Eliminate all potential dangers from the home before they become problems. Select a safe room or crate for confinement. Remove and safeguard anything in the house that the dog could chew or swallow that may be of danger such as these:

- Cleaning compounds, bug sprays, rodent poisons, antifreeze drippings, electrical cords, wires, medicines and mothballs.
- Dispose of chicken or turkey bones in a safe manner. Do not give them to your pet. Never give your dog small, sharp bones.
- Safeguard all pencils, pins and knitting needles. They can be harmful.
- Leave toilet lids down.
- Close all cabinets and closets.
- Keep windows closed or screened.
- Consult with your veterinarian about using flea dips before 15 weeks of age.
- Keep your puppy away from toxic plants.
- Make sure the place where you keep your dog when you are gone is safe and all valuable objects are out of harm's way.
- Check to see that fencing is secure. Ideally, a fence or dog run should be 5-6 feet high. The bottom 6 inches should be sunk in the ground. Use concrete bricks or patio stones to prevent digging under the fence.
- Indoor plants should be up and out of reach of the puppy.

Receiving Your Dog at the Shelter

Try to pick your dog up at the start of a weekend or vacation so you will have time to spend with your new family member. Make sure you have a good buckle collar and leash and bring them to the shelter. Put your identification on the dog immediately (the dog may get loose and take off). Try to gather all information and history (if available) on the dog, such as vaccinations, birth date, medical history, breed, reason for surrender, spay/neuter, license and any contract of ownership.

When you leave the shelter keep the dog on a lead. Be cautious about letting the dog put its head out the window of the car (it could jump out and be gone). Make sure the dog does not dart out an opened door. It will take a while for the dog to adjust.

Homecoming for Your Adopted Dog

The most important time in a newly adopted shelter dog's life is the first few weeks. When you get home, your new family member may be shy, confused and disoriented. He has gone through a lot. He will probably still be under stress. He may jump on your furniture, bark, urinate indoors, or show a number of signs of bad manners. He may try to run away. As an adopted dog, he will be especially sensitive to any correction. Don't worry This goes away. The first 48 hours are the most trying. Be watchful. Expect a few problems. This is a period of adjustment. With time, patience, persistence and understanding, he will soon get the message and learn to adjust. But for now, he needs you to teach him what is expected. Show him where he is to sleep, where he eats and where he can get fresh water. Take him to a selected spot outdoors to relieve himself every two hours. Do not give your dog unsupervised freedom at this time. Select a safe place for confinement. Spend quality time by taking him for long walks and periodic play sessions. Don't allow children to overwhelm him with too much excitement and handling. Most dogs will adjust within a couple of weeks; some take longer. Give your dog at least 6 to 12 weeks to fully adjust to his new home.

Attention — Not Too Much, Not Too Little

In the initial period, your new dog will cherish every moment it spends with you. Dogs that have been rehomed have a tendency to be insecure and cling to their new owners. They can follow you around like the proverbial puppy dog. This is because they are social, sentient beings and their kennel experience has deprived them of social interaction. Their confidence needs to be rebuilt, and, with time, it will be. Right now you need to be careful of a few things. Sooner or later you will be separated. The dog could find it hard to cope without you and might become emotionally upset. It might be fearful of being abandoned again. The dog could manifest a number of problems like barking, chewing, whining, housesoiling that all stem from this emotional anxiety. Here are some tips to deal effectively with this situation:

- Don't allow your dog unsupervised freedom at first. Don't leave him alone in the back yard. Your new dog must be taught right from wrong, and you must be with him to observe, correct and instruct.

- At first, interact with the dog only when you choose the time. Ignore the dog when he demands attention. This will help desensitize the dog and help establish you as pack leader.
- Don't make a big fuss on your arrivals and departures. Allow the dog to settle down after you arrive home.
- Your goal is to build the dog's confidence. He must believe that when you go away, it's not forever, you're coming back. It's OK.

See Separation Anxiety: A Common Problem.

Photo by Click, the Photo Connection

Introducing Your New Dog To ...

Another Family Dog

Before you bring a new dog home it is very important to carefully consider the first meeting with your current dog. Don't treat this lightly. This can be crucial and set the tone of the relationship with your current dog. Consider living space and combinations of dominant or submissive personalities before you acquire a dog.

Introduce new dogs outside on neutral ground to avoid initial territorial disputes. Use positive reinforcement. Introduce dogs on loose leashes in a neutral area. The dogs will use their body language to establish hierarchy. Maintain loose leashes at all times. Some may play bow and romp around together. This is a good sign. Give verbal praise to adult dogs for positive behavior. Take the dogs for a walk together before you bring them inside.

Use a happy, positive tone of voice to show you are pleased with any positive behavior. When you return home, let the dogs run around together in your back yard while dragging a leash that is connected to a buckle collar, and let them settle any differences themselves unless they threaten life and limb. When it is time to go inside, introduce your new dog to your home while still on a leash. Make sure you do not show partiality. Feed both at the same time and in separate food dishes. Make sure your original dog does not perceive a lack of attention.

Will there be enough space for each dog to have a retreat? If the newcomer is a puppy, the adjustment is usually smooth. Give adult dogs some quiet time away from the new puppy and some individual attention. If the newcomer is fully grown, you have to proceed with more caution.

The best combination for dogs living together is any two dogs that have been spayed or neutered, ideally a neutered male and a spayed female. Trickier are two intact females, because they often don't get along. More difficult are two intact males, because sooner or later they will try to establish dominance by fighting. Try to determine if the breed profile suggests dog dominance. Avoid the combination of two dominant dogs or dogs whose breed tends to be aggressive toward other dogs. After a little jousting they will soon establish who is dominant and submissive and get along very well. It is important that you recognize the hierarchy and that you don't try to change it. If after an extended period of time the dogs continue to fight and the fights are threatening to their health, you may have to give one of them up.

A Family Cat

Before you adopt, try to determine the dog's history of living with cats. Do not try to force the situation. At first, your cat will be apprehensive at the sight of your adopted dog. It might become agitated and run and hide. The animals will eventually make peace if they perceive there is no danger. When the cat has calmed, bring it to a high place where the dog cannot reach it. Always use a happy, soothing tone of'voice. Give the cat its favorite food treat. The dog should be curious and come up to you. Talk to them and try to give both equal, affectionate attention. Do not allow the dog to establish a pattern of chasing.

A New Infant

It is vitally important for the welfare of your dog that you manage the initial meeting with a baby successfully. Most dogs are curious about infants. They should adapt quickly and easily to the presence of a new baby. Rarely does a dog become aggressive, but since the consequences of a problem can be severe, you should observe safety precautions. A baby might be accidentally hurt when a dog becomes excited and cannot be controlled.

Before your child arrives home, teach your dog obedience commands to control it in exciting situations. Make sure your dog knows the down/stay command. Practice this before your child arrives. When your dog becomes excited, place him in a down/stay or use the step-on-the-leash exercise discussed in the training section.

Familiarize your dog with babies before you bring yours home. Invite friends who have babies to your house to accustom your dog to infants. Let your dog see you hold the child. Let him sniff the baby scent. Try to acquaint him with a baby's cry.

Attention is the key. If your dog senses a lack of attention and correlates that with the arrival of your infant, then you are inviting trouble. Try to maintain your dog's routine of meals and exercise. Try not to isolate the dog when friends or relatives come over to visit. Remember that a dog is a social animal. Perhaps a neighborhood youngster might walk and play with the dog during the hospital stay and the first couple of weeks.

When you bring your baby home, greet the dog without the baby present. Use a reassuring tone of voice. Allow the dog to sniff the smell of the baby on you or an article of clothing. After the excitement has decreased and the dog appears relaxed, gradually introduce the baby.

The dog should be on a leash, one parent attending to the dog, the other the baby. Place your dog in a sit/stay position approximately 10 to 15 feet from the baby. If the dog appears calm and under control, slowly bring the baby to the dog and allow the dog to sniff (at a safe distance). Reward the dog.

Try to consciously give the dog attention. Never leave your dog alone with your infant. Try to include the dog in everyday activities with the infant and when family and friends come to visit. The mistake most people make is to isolate the dog because of the demands of the new child. If you introduce the child in a positive way, using a pleased tone of voice, the dog should accept the child as part of the pack.

Note: If your dog is possessive around its food or toys, see the article in the behavior section of this book. You should make sure you modify this behavior.

A Young Child

In this situation, you need to teach the child as well as the dog what is expected. Children need to learn how to handle a dog, and the dog needs to know how to behave around children.

A dog generally will not accept leadership from a child. Your pup will view your children as littermates. Be cautious. Play between children and dogs should be supervised by adults. Do not permit roughhousing, chasing or wrestling games, which encourage the pup to be more oral, excited and fight against you. Children sometimes view the dog as a toy. They must be taught not to ride the dog like a horse, pull on its ears, slap, tease, punch and generally mistreat the dog. Some dogs can handle it, others get nasty. Dogs can become withdrawn, nervous, irritable, defensive and possibly aggressive if the child persists. Most dogs will give a warning to back off. Unfortunately, there are countless number of dogs that have lost their lives because of children's unwitting abuse that led to bites.

Teach your children to be kind, gentle and respectful of the dog. Let them know that the dog has feelings just like they do and rough treatment will hurt the dog. In so doing, you will be teaching your child the true meaning of caring for a living creature.

Never startle a sleeping dog or try to take its possessions or food. Include your children in obedience lessons if they are old enough so they will understand dogs. Do not leave your new dog in the company of children unchaperoned.

Photo by Sumner Fowler, Marin Humane Society

Safety — Ten Do's and Don'ts for Children

Children are the most frequent victims of dog attacks. Dog attacks are the number one reported health problem for children in the United States. It is imperative that you teach your children how to behave around dogs. Not all dogs are friendly. Make sure your dog is spayed or neutered. The Centers for Disease Control in a 1994 study found that biters tended to be male and unneutered, and were more likely to live at the home of the bitten child.

1. Don't approach dogs you don't know without the permission of the owner. Not all dogs are friendly and some may bite.
2. If adults tell you it is OK to pet their dog…
   Do not run toward the dog or scream.
   Do not hug, poke, grab or pound on the dog's head.
   Do approach slowly and quietly.
   Do allow the dog to sniff your hand first.
   Do pet the dog gently under his chin or on his chest.
3. Do not attempt to touch or pet any dog that growls, snarls or runs away from you.
4. Do not play roughly with any dog.

5. Do not try to pet a dog through fences, car windows or cages. Do not approach a dog that is tied up.
6. Do not attempt to take bones, food or toys from a dog.
7. Do not frighten or startle any dog, especially when it is sleeping.
8. Do not attempt to punish a dog in any way.
9. If a dog you don't know comes up to you...
   Do not run or yell.
   Do not look directly at him.
   Do stand perfectly still.
   Do watch the dog out of the corner of your eye.
   Do walk away slowly after a minute or two.
10. Do treat all dogs, cats and other animals kindly and humanely.

Crates and Confinement Areas

Dogs recently adopted from shelters need the feeling of shelter and sanctuary that a crate or confined area can provide. THIS IS NOT A JAIL! Crates and confinement areas not only serve as a place to sleep, but they also can be a positive tool in training to PREVENT problems from occurring.

Most owners are unable to supervise constantly. Crates and confinement areas provide a safe place where dogs can't get in trouble. They can't chew your couch, destroy your personal belongings, relieve themselves or hurt themselves by chewing hazardous plants or materials.

Crates can aid in allowing the dog to sleep inside the home and preferably inside the master bedroom. Crates simulate a den. A den to a dog is a place that provides protection from predators and the elements, a sanctuary where he feels safe and secure. A crate should fit the fully grown dog so he is able to stand up and turn around and lie down full length. If you buy a crate for a puppy in anticipation of his mature size, place a cardboard box inside to take up the excessive room. This will prevent the dog from soiling on one side and lying on the other. Never confine the dog for more than four hours in a crate.

Other methods of confinement where the dog is free to walk around are:

- A safe room.
- An open area in your home that is cordoned off by using a baby gate.
- A sturdy wire pen that forms a circle six feet in diameter or can be used similar to a baby gate for wide expanses.

Sleeping

Try to have the dog sleep within close range of your bedroom or in your bedroom. According to a 1994 survey on pet ownership 64% of dog owners allow their pets to sleep indoors, 18% on the bed, 20% in a pet bed, 25% on the floor. Thirty-six percent choose to have their dog sleep outside.

Sleeping on the owner's bed is not recommended. It will undermine your leadership and authority. A dog should always have its own bed. The bed should be comfortable and fit the dog when it is fully grown. Bedding materials should be washable. Use a lamb's wool pad or other suitable bed that provides cushioned support. A crate is ideal. Dogs like to sleep with their back abutting a hard surface. The area should be clean, dry and free of drafts. Your dog's bed is an important place for him. Include an old blanket or large towel. Establish a routine bedtime. Dogs love regularity. Sleep is as essential for dogs as it is for all creatures. A puppy will require more sleep than an adult dog. A dog will sometimes twitch its limbs and make little whimper noises during deep sleep — it's normal.

How to Train a Dog to Enjoy a Confinement Area

First, a dog must be taught to enjoy the confined area or crate. Start forming positive associations with the space by giving him dog treats and feeding your dog in the confined area without closing or shutting him in. DON'T FORCE HIM. Let him take it slowly. Do this for three or four days. He may be shy at first. Once he is accustomed and unafraid, make him stay in the confined area by restraining him at the door with your hand for a few minutes. Praise him and give him some treats. Repeat this a few times. Gradually increase the time. Make sure you praise him! Once he is comfortable with this, restrain him by closing the door while using praise. Eventually, the dog will sit quietly and sleep with the door closed. The dog should think that being confined is not going to last forever. Make this a pleasant experience. Avoid negative associations. Do not always leave the house when you place your dog in the confined area (you don't want your dog to associate your leaving with being in confinement). Don't release your dog from the confinement when it barks, only when it is quiet.

When using a crate, if you are going to be gone for an extended time (more than 3 hours), arrange for someone to let your dog out. Don't use housetraining pads inside the crate. Never punish your dog by putting him in the confined area. As the dog matures and your confidence in him grows, you can entrust him with more freedom.

Feeding Your New Dog

Changes in food should be gradual and take place over a 3- to 5-day span. Inquire as to the kind of food your dog was fed in the shelter. If you plan to change dog food, introduce one-third of the new with two-thirds of the old shelter food for two days, followed by two-thirds of the new with one-third of the old for two days. Then start feeding all of the new food on the fifth day.

Feeding time is the highlight of the dog's day. Dogs are entirely dependent on their owners to provide a balanced diet that meets all of their nutritional requirements. Feed your dog the highest quality dog food you can afford. A dry kibble-type food is best. All dogs are individuals and their needs may vary depending on activity, breed and age. Feed for 30 minutes per feeding then remove the food. Don't leave food out all day. When dogs are free to eat at any time it's hard to establish regularity. These dogs are prone to obesity. Have regular times of the day for feeding. Try not to feed after 6 or 7 p.m. Do not feed for one hour before or after strenuous exercise. The dog should always have clean water available.

If you have more than one dog, feed both simultaneously. If you have a long-legged dog, place the food on a low bench. This aids in digestion. If your dog refuses food for more than 24 hours consult your veterinarian. Don't feed before car travel.

Puppy Feeding

Food manufacturers offer food for different stages of a dog's life. They believe nutritional needs change as they grow, so there are different foods for puppies, for mature dogs, for extra-active dogs and for adult dogs. Foods designed for puppies are higher in fat (to meet their high-energy needs), higher in protein and fortified with vitamins and minerals to enhance growth and development. Puppy food is specially formulated for dogs until they reach maturity (the larger the dog the longer they take to mature). A general rule for puppies is to feed smaller portions more often but don't exceed their daily caloric requirement. For puppies less than three months of age, you may prefer to soften their dry food with a little warm water. There is current debate over the merits of specially formulated puppy food. Consult your veterinarian for the type of food and schedule they recommend.

Age	Number of Meals
3 weeks to 3 months	4 meals a day
3 months to 6 months	3 meals a day
6 months to 1 year	2 meals a day
1 year and up	1 or 2 meals a day (1/2 daily amount if 2)

Hear our humble prayer, O God, for our friends the animals, especially for animals who are suffering, for any that are hunted or lost or deserted or frightened or hungry, for all that must be put to death. We entreat for them all Thy mercy and pity, and for those who deal with them we ask a heart of compassion and gentle hands and kindly words. Make us, ourselves, to be true friends to animals.

Albert Schweitzer

Training a Shelter Dog

A Prescription for Success

A study that examined successful shelter adoptions found that people who are successful:

- Possessed a quiet confidence and flexibility. They didn't get overly excited when their dog displayed unacceptable behavior.
- Were inclined to try to understand the thinking behind the dog's actions.
- Had a tolerance for the dog's natural tendencies, like pet hairs or paw prints on the kitchen floor.
- Had a sense of responsibility and the desire to work out any problem. "I adopted the dog. Now it's my responsibility."
- Had a reasonable expectation that it would take time for the dog to adjust to its new home.
- Were aware of training techniques and the need for retraining.
- Were able to cope with the costs of owning a dog and related expenses like training classes.

Training Goals

The ultimate goal of dog training is to have a better relationship with your dog. You want a well-behaved, good-natured, responsive companion that blends into your home and community. In order to train your adopted dog and deal successfully with problems you, the owner(s), must become trained. This is easy to do if you learn some basic principles and establish leadership. Your responsibility for training begins when you get your dog. Your dog's life depends on it.

The Way Dogs Think

Photo by David Jensen, Alaska Pet-ography

If you've ever watched a litter of pups at play, you'll recall the pups jumped and nipped one another. Some were pushier than others. What you observed was the forming of a pecking order. The pups instinctively know that a hierarchy must be established for the survival and safety of the pack. These patterns of behavior have evolved from the wolf. By understanding these behaviors we can learn to deal effectively with domestic dogs.

When the new pup is brought into a human household the instinct does not change. It is still a member of a pack, in this case, the human pack. You must take over as leader and teach the pup that he falls below humans in his new pack. The pup will accept and be comfortable with the lowest position as long as you are a kind, strong, firm and consistent leader. To fail means the dog will assume he or she is the leader. You will find the dog will be very difficult to control. Obedience commands are the primary tool used to establish leadership. Anything your pup wants or needs must be earned by obeying a command (sit). Nothing in life is free. This is difficult because it is natural for us to give our dogs food, petting and attention without thinking about it. However, this indiscriminate attention sends the dog the message that he is the dominant member of the pack. Leaders eat first. Feed your dog after you eat. Leaders enter and exit a door first. Use a leash or command to have your dog wait until you invite your dog to follow you out the door. A dog that perceives himself as dominant over you is certainly not going to be easily trained and may cause you some serious problems. Practicing obedience commands will firmly establish you as the leader of the pack.

The Right Approach

Dogs love to learn. Training your dog helps you gain control and gives you the ability to communicate what is, and what is not expected so that your dog can live harmoniously in your home. In teaching dogs, leadership and authority are the secrets of success. You must establish your authority and leadership and communicate with your dog in a positive manner. There are many different ways to train a dog. The old way of training used punishment and force to compel the dog to obey. Today, modern trainers have discovered a more successful and humane way of training, using positive reinforcement methods that emphasize PRAISE. "Good Dog!" This method makes training easy and enjoyable for both you and your dog. It's more motivating for the dog and it minimizes stress. It is imperative that you use positive reinforcement with a dog adopted from a shelter. Hitting, heavy leash jerking and other forms of punishment are counterproductive. If you learn how and when to praise effectively and how to properly correct your dog, you will have at your fingertips the primary means of communication with your pet. Praise is the language of dogs — and people.

What Is Positive Reinforcement?

It is vitally important that you understand the concept of positive reinforcement and how it applies to training a shelter dog. Positive reinforcement was introduced to the world by B. F. Skinner, a psychologist and learning theorist. His major finding relating to dogs is that learned behavior will be more readily retained and repeated if it is reinforced (benefits the animal). You can apply this principle to teach your dog how to do what he is told. The desired behavior will become a pleasurable, positive experience your dog will enjoy and repeat. Positive reinforcement will become an effective, nonconfrontational means of building your leadership.

Positive reinforcement is illustrated in a situation where you noticed your dog had to relieve himself. Instead of any reprimand or physical correction, you take him outside to the appropriate spot and praise him continuously throughout the act of relieving himself and show him how happy you are with his behavior. In effect, you are making all desirable behaviors rewarding to your dog through the use of intermittent rewards such as praise, petting, food or play. You are using praise to motivate. This encourages your dog to repeat the action.

Different Ways of Correcting a Dog

Instructive Correction

This is a correction applied at the commencement of, or during, an unwanted behavior that persuades the dog to adopt a previously taught correct behavior. Instructive corrections can only be effective if your dog was previously taught what is correct for him to do. If you did not catch the dog in the act, forget it. It's too late. In the future remember to prevent negative behaviors from occurring and reinforce all positive behaviors.

Example: When you catch the dog in the act of wetting on the living room carpet you say, "NO (corrective)! Outside (instructive)!"

This would stop the dog in the act and remind him he has been taught to go outside to relieve himself. You then take him outside to finish his business.

Corrections

Corrections should be given at the precise moment an unwanted behavior occurs to tell the dog his behavior is unacceptable. It can be physical (given through a training collar and leash, only) or verbal (using a low guttural sound like **URAGH** or a sharp **NO**). Corrections will stop or interrupt a behavior from occurring and tell the dog that what he is doing at the time is wrong. **By itself, it probably will not eliminate the behavior or teach him an acceptable behavior**.

An example of a correction would be when a dog is urinating in front of you on the living room rug. You immediately say in a firm voice **No**! The dog stops. This does not stop the wetting in the future or teach the dog where to wet. It only stops the immediate behavior.

Punishment

Punishment is a harsh action that is taken after a wrongdoing. It will not cure an unwanted behavior because your dog will not connect what he was doing at the time with the punishment that follows. There is no instruction. It will make him suspicious and wary of you and teach him to fear you, especially if you use your hands. Punishment for a dog adopted from a shelter is especially inappropriate. Punishment tends to tear down confidence. The objective is to build confidence by reinforcing desired behavior. Punishment is very stressful for the dog, especially if the dog was never taught proper behavior. All dogs want to please their owners. Problems occur when dogs don't know how.

An example of punishment would be when a dog wets in the living room in the owner's absence. When the owner arrives home and finds the mess the dog is smacked with a newspaper or the nose of the dog is rubbed in the mess. The dog experiences no training and no learning. This teaches the dog to fear you. It becomes anxious because it does not know right from wrong. It does not know how to please you.

Proper Corrections

Dogs must have a clear idea of what it is you want them to do and the meaning of the command before any correction is administered. Use repetitions when first teaching your dog a command or exercise!

Physical corrections should only be administered through a collar and leash. A sharp tugging of the leash on the training collar should not hurt the dog but act as a deterrent to let the dog know he has erred.

Never discipline or punish after the fact. It's too late. Dogs live in the here and now. Corrections or positive reinforcement must occur as the behavior is exhibited. A delay of two seconds reduces effectiveness. Proper corrections begins with the lowest intensity necessary to get the message across. If corrections are not properly used, the dog becomes accustomed and it becomes increasingly difficult to administer an effective correction. Never hit or strike a shelter dog. Physical discipline seldom solves behavior problems and, in fact, frequently causes some very serious problems. For a number of reasons, punishment is an ineffective and often counterproductive method of changing behavior. A far better approach to obtaining good behavior from your dog is to *prevent* inappropriate behavior and train and reward appropriate behavior.

If you arrive home to find your dog has engaged in bad behavior, DO NOT PUNISH. Count to ten and forget it. Many people think dogs are repentant because they see a submissive posture. This submissive posture is a reaction to the threatening body language of an upset owner.

Training With Food

The most important part of training is to reward the dog for good behavior. Tiny morsels of food are used as rewards to reinforce teachings and encourage the desired behaviors to be repeated. Trainers use food to lure the dogs into proper position and direct the dog's movements without unnecessary pulling, tugging, yanking or leash jerking. The dog isn't coerced and punished and it willingly complies. Random food rewards are used to convey to the dog the trainer's pleasure in its behavior and at the same time reward it for performance. The dog is forming positive associations with its trainer. The best reasons for using random food rewards as a training aid lies in its ability to reinforce positive behavior, motivate your dog to enjoy working for you and reduce the stress inherent in training.

Detractors of food training will say they don't always want to carry food around when they want to give their dog a command. They miss the point entirely. We first teach the dog what is expected, using many repetitions and intermittent rewards. This reinforces teaching and encourages the desired behavior to be repeated. Other reward methods that are used with success are verbal praise using a high-pitched, happy voice, petting or stroking, attention and play.

Use small tidbits (about the size of a bean) of soft food like cooked hot dogs or liver treats. Give the treat at the exact moment the desired behavior occurs. Always couple food rewards with verbal praise and/or petting. Food rewards work best when the dog is hungry. Don't overfeed with treats. Figure out your dog's daily caloric needs and use part of that allotment for training with food treats.

Eliminating the Food Reward

Make sure your dog has a good understanding of the exercises before you phase out food treats. Rewards should be given on a random basis (like a slot machine). Start reducing the frequency of the rewards slowly, over a period of weeks.

Consistency Is Essential

There is nothing more confusing to a dog than inconsistent treatment. Do you say no while someone else in the household says OK? If there are no clear-cut rules, the only possible result is misunderstanding. This will set your training back. Make sure everyone in the household agrees on the rules, then follow through EVERY TIME!

Communication

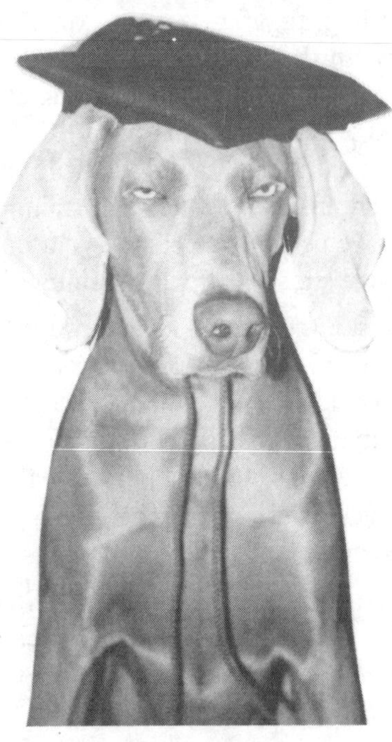

We communicate with dogs using body language and verbal sounds and tones. It is important to know your dog's body language and what its posture means. Verbal sounds or commands are most commonly used in training.

It's OK to talk to your dog. Work at using different tones of your voice. The tone of your voice is more important than words. Use a happy, high-pitched voice when praising. Use a low, guttural sound to show disapproval. Give commands like you mean it, and then, if necessary, follow through. When you give your dog a command or correct him for anything you must be able to enforce what you say. If you give him a command to sit and he chooses not to, you must immediately place him in a sit. If you do not, you have effectively taught him that your command means nothing. Once the command is successful, praise. Avoid whining or pleading with your dog and saying **no, no, no, no ...**

Training Equipment

The equipment used in training is very important:

- Medium link steel or nylon slip collar (puppies use nylon buckle collars only) while training, otherwise a buckle collar. The collar should be placed high on the neck and fit the neck with two inches to spare. To properly use a training collar, face the dog and form the letter "P" with the training collar. Place the collar over the dog's head. If the collar is properly fit and placed on the dog, it should release immediately after a sharp tug on the leash.
- A 4-foot to 6-foot leather or nylon leash.

- A 20-foot to 30-foot nylon long line.
- Soft food treats cut to the size of a bean.
- Safe toy.

Before You Begin Training

- Because everything your dog does is rewarding in some way, allowing undesirable behaviors to occur is the same as training them. Supervise until the dog earns more trust.
- In order to build reliability, it is necessary to train in multiple locations. Begin with conditions that present very low levels of distraction, like a hallway or room. Once the exercises are successful and you are confident of the dog's ability, proceed to more distracting conditions. (Dogs are excited by movement.)
- Dogs learn best by working for a few minutes at a time, several times per day if possible.
- Be firm and exacting in your training sessions but keep them lively and fun. Finish each session on a positive note and follow with a brief play period.
- Be prepared for occasional bad days. Dogs have them too!
- The four P's of training are: Patience, Persistence, Practice and lots of Praise.

The Commands

Sit Using the Food Method

Start by placing the dog in front of you, holding a piece of food just above your dog's nose (not too high or this will cause the dog to jump). Slowly bring the food back toward the tail and give the single command **SIT**. It may be necessary to place your hand behind the dog to prevent rear movement. At the precise second the dog sits, praise him using a happy, high-pitched voice and give him a small soft food treat. Release him with your chosen release word. Repeat five times per session.

Photo by Click, the Photo Connection

Sit Using the Physical Placement Method

For puppies, start by placing your dog at your left side facing the same direction. Place the dog in the sit position by pulling up on the collar while gently tucking your hand behind the dog's knees. As the rump hits the ground say **SIT**! Do not include the dog's name in the command. Praise your dog then release him using a release word. Repeat five times per session.

For adult dogs, give the command **SIT.** At the same time pull up on the leash with your right hand while gently pushing down on his rear with your left hand. The instant he sits praise him using a high, happy voice. Release him with your release word. Repeat five times per session.

The Release Word

Choose a word such as *OK*, *free*, *break*, *up* and use the word consistently to release the dog from a command. Try to use a neutral tone to your voice when you use the release word. It is extremely important that rewards and praise be given BEFORE the release word. It is important for the dog to form positive association with the act of obedience, not the release.

Sit/Stay

Place your dog in a sit. Position the dog on your left side, facing the same way. As you give the verbal command **STAY**, give a hand signal by bringing your right hand, palm open, down in front of the dog's face. Pivot in front of your dog while holding the leash.

The command must be in a firm voice. If your dog stays in place for just a few seconds, release him. Gradually lengthen the time to ten seconds, then thirty seconds and build on success. If the dog attempts to get up, in a serious tone of voice say, **SIT** (instructive reprimand), **STAY** (instruction) and immediately place the dog back into position. (The dog will think, "Oh she really did mean sit.") Praise and then release upon successful achievement. Do not repeat the command more than once! Place your dog in the sit. Talk to your dog. Say GOOD **SIT/STAY** in a pleased tone of voice when your dog is sitting and staying. Puppies have short attention spans. Don't demand a long stay from them. Repeat five successful times each session.

Down

Place your dog in a sit on your left side facing the same direction as yourself. Kneel next to your dog. With your left hand gently on the back collar, hold a tidbit of food at the dog's eye level. Bring your right hand down and into the dog (directly under his chest) with your palm down to the floor. Make the motion quickly and give the command **DOWN**. Give the dog the treat immediately when it lies down. Use your release word. Bring the dog into a sit position and repeat five successful times. Note: Your hand motion will eventually become a hand signal for down.

Down/Stay

When the dog is in the down position, give a hand signal by bringing your right hand, palm open, down in front of the dog's face and give the verbal command **STAY**. Pivot in front of the dog. If the dog breaks, return the dog to the down position and repeat the command. Start with small time intervals and build on success. Limit your movements and stay close at first, then gradually increase your distance when you are confident the dog knows the command. Talk to your dog. Say **GOOD DOWN STAY** while it is performing successfully. Require your dog to perform a 10- to 15-minute down/stay per day, especially if your dog is inappropriately excited.

The Stand

Place your dog on your left side. The leash should be in your right hand. Place your left hand, palm facing forward, in front of your dog's rear legs. With your right hand, pull forward, parallel to the ground and give the command **STAND**. Your left hand should prevent the dog from moving forward or sitting. Hold the position for ten seconds saying, **GOOD STAND**. Reward with tiny, soft food treats. Use your release command word. Repeat five successful times per session.

Stand/Stay

When the dog is in the standing position on your left, give a hand signal by bringing your right hand, palm open, down in front of the dog's face and the command **STAY**. Limit your movements at first. Start with short time intervals of ten seconds and build on success. Work up to two minutes. If your dog breaks, say **NO**! and reposition your dog in the stand position, then say, **STAND** (in a firm voice), and repeat the hand signal and command, **STAY**. Say, **GOOD STAND / STAY** while the dog is succeeding. Reward the dog upon successful completion with a food treat and repeat five successful times per session.

Recall

Attach a 30-foot-long line to the dog's collar. While a helper gently restrains the dog by the chest, show him you have a piece of food and then move about twelve feet away. Your right hand is brought up in an arc from your right side away from your body to shoulder height and then continuing in one motion toward the left side of your chest. Call your dog by his name followed by the command **COME**. Back-pedal or turn and run away from your dog. When your dog reaches you, stop and face him and reward him with lots of praise and a morsel of food. Make the game fun. Build on success. Start in an area where there are no distractions. Gradually work at a greater distance and around distractions. Once the response is predictable, use random food rewards and then slowly eliminate the food rewards. Avoid calling your dog and then correcting him. Always praise your dog when he comes to you after you call him. Avoid doing anything negative when practicing the recall. If your dog is off leash and you call him and he doesn't come, do not repeat the command. Physically go to him and place him on a leash. Go back to basics.

Step on the Leash

This exercise is used as a means of establishing leadership and control without direct confrontation. It is not meant for all dogs. Take caution when using this exercise. If strong dogs resist, they can upend the handler. Slightly built handlers should not use this exercise. If the dog becomes overexcited, do not continue with the exercise. Do this exercise at home, in a quiet area.

Attach a leash to your dog's buckle collar. Step down on the leash close to the snap. This puts your dog in a position where it is uncomfortable to sit or stand. It must lie down. If your dog struggles or resists, let him. DO NOT discipline, look at, talk to, or touch the dog. As your dog learns to accept the position, slowly move your foot up the leash a few inches from the snap to allow head movement. If your dog attempts to stand, move your foot back close to the snap. To release, simply step off the leash. Do not use a release word, pet or praise.

Begin the exercise during quiet times for a few minutes, a few time each day. Gradually increase the time. Use the exercise for control at the veterinary office, during dinner time, or at any time you want the dog to settle down.

Off

The **OFF** command is used to tell your dog what is not acceptable. It is a very useful command in a number of situations because you are communicating the distinction between acceptable and unacceptable action. The command helps reaffirm your leadership and strengthens the meaning of your release command.

With your dog on a leash and using a training collar, place a desirable piece of food on the floor in front of your dog. The moment the dog attempts to take the food, give a correction, and, at the same time, give the firm command **OFF**. Repeat the command and, if necessary, the leash correction until the dog no longer attempts to take the food. When the dog no longer attempts to take the food, give him your release word and then allow him to take the food.

Walking on the Leash and Leash Pulling

A positive association with the leash must be made so that the dog will not perceive the leash as a shackle. To accomplish this, let the dog wear the leash around the home on a *buckle* collar for a couple of days while supervised. Do this in a spirit of play for short intervals. Once the dog accepts the leash dragging along, pick up the end and follow him. Encourage the dog to follow you. Walk at a fast pace with the least possible amount of pressure on the leash. Praise the dog for walking along nicely. Never allow the dog to pull. If the dog pulls or becomes distracted, say NO PULL and turn and walk briskly in the opposite direction. When he catches up to you, praise him in a happy, high-pitched voice. Repeat this anytime the dog pulls. Another way is to simply stop when your dog pulls on the leash and continue after the leash slackens. You must be consistent. If the problem persists, consider the use of the HALTI™ or Promise™

collar. This collar acts on the same principle as a horse collar. It is very gentle and humane.

Proofing

Proofing is used after a command is thoroughly taught and practiced using numerous repetitions. Be sure the dog knows the command. Proofing is a controlled training situation where you are in a position to administer a leash correction the instant your dog breaks the command. For example, with your dog at your left side, give the dog the command **SIT/STAY**. Have a friend entice the dog with a tennis ball or other desirable object to break the command. If the dog does not break the command, bravo; if it does, administer a correction the instant the dog breaks. Then say, **NO**, **SIT/STAY** while placing him in proper position. Then verbally reward him saying, **GOOD SIT / STAY**. Dogs must be trained in different locations with a variety of distractions. Always start with the lowest level of distraction and slowly progress to higher levels.

Puppy Training for the Adopted Puppy

Photo by Sumner Fowler, Marin Humane Society

Behavior problems kill more dogs than disease or accidents combined. In many ways puppyhood is the most important time of a dog's life, a time when experiences are new and have a long-lasting effect on shaping the dog's future personality.

If you have adopted a shelter puppy you should pay heed to this crucial period of development in the life of the dog. This is the most important time to influence the proper development of behavior. It is much, much easier to prevent problems from developing than it is to attempt to cure them once they have become firmly entrenched. The earlier you start working with your dog the better.

The best time for puppy class is between 10 and 18 weeks and after the second vaccination. The class should be held in a controlled environment to prevent sickness. Your veterinarian should approve.

It is important that positive associations and impressions be made with people, places and things in the environment and with humans and other dogs during this imprint period. Dogs that are isolated during these critical weeks may become fearful and/or aggressive and are unable, during the entire course of their lives, to handle new people or situations normally. Provide contact with as many different types of people as possible — men, women, children, teenagers, oldsters and quiet or loud people — as soon as your dog has received its vaccinations against disease. Expose it to parks, shopping centers, street noises and busy sidewalks. Avoid isolating it in yards or chaining it in the back yard.

Your puppy should receive temperament training that is designed to build its confidence and prevent future behavior problems, while inhibiting and channeling the biting instinct into more positive outlets. According to Dr. Ian Dunbar, a noted dog behaviorist, "in the world of domestic dogs, the puppy is usually removed from its natural sources of information at about eight weeks and in most cases finds itself the only dog in a human den. At eight weeks the puppy is not prepared to deal with the world at large. It thus becomes a human responsibility to continue the pup's education. Failure to do so results in the puppy's inability to adapt to its environment, or at least to adapt in a harmonious way with its human pack members." The class should teach you about dog behaviors and help you deal with any problem behaviors. The class should be held in a clean environment to guard against infectious disease. Consult with your veterinarian for a recommended trainer.

Do not use a training collar (choke collar) until after the age of five months.

Basic Home Obedience Classes

Every dog should know basic commands such as sit, stay, down, stand, heel and come. Your dog should also learn the meaning of NO and OK and be taught not to pull on the leash. Your dog should be able to do these things in any circumstance or situation, not just at home. A training class will provide a place of learning in a distracting environment. You receive hands-on instruction from experienced professionals. Take a class and choose a trainer who emphasizes the use of positive reinforcement such as verbal praise, play or treats. You should look for a class where the instructor teaches not only basic commands, but dog behavior as well. Make sure you inform the instructor of any special behavioral tendency the dog may exhibit.

Choosing a Trainer

For the first-time dog owner, there is nothing more important than choosing the right instructor to help you through the training process. You need to decide exactly what you want to train your dog to do. Do you want your dog to be a well-behaved companion or do you want to obtain an obedience or conformation title?

Look for a trainer who specializes in a given area. All dogs and dog owners can improve their relationship with basic dog obedience training. The biggest difference in trainers is the use of corrections. Some trainers teach emphasizing positive reinforcement methods using praise and food, while others use coercion with various intensity.

Meaning should be understood by the dog before the use of punishment or corrections. Positive training and motivational methods place a minimum amount of stress on the dog.

The best method of finding a trainer is word-of-mouth. A good trainer will have an excellent reputation. Select two or three well-referred trainers and ask them the following questions.

Ten Questions You Should Ask a Potential Trainer

1. How do you correct a dog?
2. What methods do you use?
3. Do you use force? If so, how severe?
4. How would you deal with an aggressive dog?
5. How would you train a shelter dog ?
6. Do you use prong collars, shock collars, choke collars, head harnesses, nylon slip collars or buckle collars?
7. Do you use dominance techniques? Explain. (Dominance techniques like scruff shakes where you grab the back of the dog's head and violently shake, alpha rollovers where you pin

and hold a dog on his back in a submissive posture and hanging, where you lift him off his feet until he almost passes out should be avoided, especially with shelter dogs).

8. How long have you been in business?
9. How many students are in your classes?
10. Ask if you can monitor a class, and if you can, observe how the trainer works with the students. In the class, does the trainer explain carefully what is going on, what to expect, and how to do it? Does each student get the attention needed? Are the trainer methods humane?

Remember, trainers train people to train their dogs. A trainer should have good communication skills. There are many trainers who know a lot about dogs but have a hard time communicating their knowledge. Dog training is both an art and a science that requires using the proper technique for a particular dog temperament. The object of training is to establish a better relationship with your dog. Commands are not an end in themselves, but a means to bring about a better companion dog.

I recommend to those people of either sex, whose courage is inclined to fail them if they are long alone, who are rather frightened in the evenings if there is nobody to speak to, who don't like putting out their own lights and climbing silently to a solitary bedroom, who are full of affection and has nothing to fasten it on to, who long to be loved, and, for whatever reason aren't I would recommend all such to go to the animal shelter and obtain a dog. There, in eager rows, they will find a choice of friends, only waiting to be given a chance of cheering and protecting. Asking nothing in return, and, whatever happens, never going to complain, never going to be cross, never going to judge, and against whom no sin committed will be too great for immediate and joyful forgiveness.

Elizabeth, Countess Russell

5

Preventing Problem Behavior

Separation Anxiety: A Common Problem

Some shelter dogs exhibit separation anxiety. This is a condition in which the dog cannot cope with the absence of its owners. Dogs are pack animals. They enjoy the company and attention of their owners and they form emotional attachments. Some shelter dogs have a severe reaction to a separation from their owner because of the experience of being relinquished. They think they are being abandoned again. They manifest their anxiety by vocalization (whining, barking, howling), destructive behavior (chewing, digging), escaping, housesoiling, and, in some severe cases, self-mutilation. Some people think the dog is "getting even" with them for leaving them alone. Or the dog was a disobedient, bad dog. Some people unwittingly punish the dog when they encounter the problem. Little did they know the reason for this behavior was the dog's strong desire to be with them and the dog's inability to adjust to the separation. Here is what you can do if your dog shows signs of separation anxiety:

- NEVER CORRECT or PUNISH a dog that exhibits separation anxiety. When you come home and punish your dog for something he did earlier, he is likely to associate the punishment with his enthusiastic greeting. Therefore, punishment only increases his anxiety. Just forget it! Focus on the positive and reward your dog using verbal praise, treats or petting. You need to build the confidence of your dog.

- Don't make a big fuss over your departures and arrivals; no long affectionate greetings or good-byes.
- Prevent problems by confining your dog to a safe area (with plenty of water) when you are not able to supervise. Provide lots of toys that satisfy the chewing instinct.
- Interact with your dog only when you choose, not because your dog demands it. Quality time with your dog is essential.
- Work with your dog using obedience commands for fifteen minutes daily to build the dog's confidence.
- Practice mock departures of varying duration (from 1 minute to 10 minutes). Use different stimuli such as grabbing your keys or starting your car. You need to let him know that when you leave, it's not forever.
- Vigorously exercise the dog for at least fifteen minutes, twice daily. The most important time to exercise is in the mornings.
- Use pet sitters, doggie day care, neighborhood friends or a teenage boy or girl who can be trusted to play, exercise and let the dog out during the day.
- Leave an old T-shirt or other old article of clothing with your scent in the dog's area.
- Leave safe toys for the dog to play with in your absence.
- Leave the radio on as a comforting sound.
- If you experience problems ask your veterinarian for a referral to an experienced behaviorist.

Taking on a shelter dog with a past is not easy. But if you have the patience and understanding to work through difficulties, the rewards of reclaiming and nurturing a life can be immeasurable.

Housetraining the Shelter Dog

Most adult dogs have been housetrained at some point in their lives. Some have been in kennels and need reminders. Play it safe and begin housetraining as soon as you bring your dog home. Treat your dog as if he was never housetrained. The goal is to teach the dog to eliminate outdoors in the same area and give you a signal that it needs to go out.

The best way to go about this is to establish a daily routine of taking your dog outside for regular walks (20 to 30 minutes), immediately after feedings, after you arrive home, after exercise and before bed. Keep a written housetraining schedule. Supervision is very important. Remember, you cannot train a dog that you are not with. Don't let your dog run unsupervised. Look for signs that the dog has to go, such as sniffing, whining, turning in circles, squatting or going to the door. Place your dog on the leash and take him to his spot. PRAISE him for successful achievement. By encouraging your pet with praise he will want to repeat the act over and over.

Teach your puppy to perform on command. Use a trigger word or phrase like **HURRY UP**. Praise him for successful achievement. Set a time limit of 3 to 5 minutes. If a dog does not do his business by then, put him back in a confined area like a crate or safe room. Repeat the process in 10 minutes.

Any excitement, such as play, may result in floor wetting. When an accident happens (and they probably will happen), never punish after the fact, especially by striking with a newspaper or rubbing his nose in it. Clean and thoroughly deodorize the entire stained area with a scent neutralizer such as a 50/50 solution of vinegar and water. Make sure you eliminate all of the scent because, if you don't, the smell may trigger a repeat act in that same spot.

The only effective correction is to catch the dog in the act. This gives you the opportunity to teach the dog where it is appropriate to relieve himself. If you see the dog about to eliminate, make a loud noise by banging on a wall or counter; when it stops, say **OUTSIDE** and immediately take it to the correct place outside. This teaches the dog that it is not the act of elimination that you are displeased with; it is the location.

Remember the keys:

- Patience
- Establish a Routine
- Reward Success
- Supervise
- Never Correct or Punish After the Fact
- Neutralize Entire Scent of Any Mistakes
- Be Consistent

Housetraining for Puppies

Photo by Click, the Photo Connectior

A puppy cannot effectively control its elimination until approximately five to six months. A young pup's bladder is not strong enough to go through the entire night without relief. The normal healthy puppy will want to relieve himself when he wakes up, after each feeding, following strenuous exercise or after any excitement.

Take the pup out before you go to bed and then confine the pup to a small area like a crate where it is comfortable and able to stand up and turn around. When you hear the pup become restless, get up and take it out. If you are a heavy sleeper, you will need to set your alarm for four to five hours after retiring. A puppy should hold it through the night around four to five months.

A crate is strongly recommended. It's very hard for most people to supervise a dog all the time. A crate allows you to confine your dog to a safe area (no more than three hours during the day) when you are unable to supervise. This prevents accidents. If you work during the day, use a puppy pen that is lined with papers. You will need to paper train or use absorbent pads until the pup is able to control its bladder for a longer time.

Chewing

Dogs chew for many reasons. For puppies, teething is a factor, along with investigation and curiosity. In adult dogs chewing may be a means of relieving monotony or stress. Our goal is not to stop the dog from chewing but to channel the behavior to appropriate objects. Dogs have a physiological need to chew. It is important for a dog to have a wide variety of safe chew objects differing in size, texture and shape. Dogs learn with more variety and stay interested longer.

Providing safe chew toys is the first step. To your dog these objects and your remote control or new pair of shoes are all objects to chew. The second step is to teach the dog what is appropriate to chew. Everything else is not permitted. Remember to PRAISE all appropriate chewing. Most owners neglect to do this and fail to take advantage of an easy and pleasant way to avoid undesirable chewing.

The third step is to prevent undesirable chewing in your absence by using a crate or confining your dog to a safe area by using a baby gate or portable dog pen. Each time your dog engages in inappropriate chewing and you are not there to correct him for it, he has learned to do it. You have actually trained the behavior by default. Even more importantly, you are risking your dog's life. Allowing a chewer to chew inappropriate objects can be deadly. Poisoning, blockages, punctured intestines and electrocution are just a few of the dire possibilities.

The fourth step is to make sure your dog is vigorously exercised or walked daily before you leave. Many dogs chew out of boredom and frustration.

Correction may be used only when you catch the dog in the act. Clap your hands, yell **HEY**, or attach a length of light cord or rope to a collar so a jerk may be given. Praise the dog the second he stops and substitute an acceptable item. Praise the dog for any attention given to the appropriate item.

Try to avoid tug-of-war games. They cause a dog to become more oral and excitable and are to be avoided.

Meal times should be on a consistent schedule to eliminate the possibility of hunger stress. Don't make a big fuss when you leave or arrive. If you find your dog has chewed something inappropriate, don't hit the dog or punish the dog. Put the dog out of sight in a safe place, clean up the mess, count to ten and act like nothing happened. At that time it is too late for any meaningful training to take place.

Once your dog has demonstrated the ability to chew only appropriate objects, you can begin to let him have more freedom. Chewing problems can be exasperating and costly; however, if you apply good prevention, correction and positive reinforcement techniques, most chewing problems will be solved. The help of a professional behaviorist may be required for severe problems.

Chew Toys

- large sterilized femur bone (fill hollow end with peanut butter)
- white unbleached flat rawhide
- knotted rope toy
- frozen carrots
- medium sized rubber ball or tennis ball
- assorted shape lamb's wool chew toys
- Kongs™
- Nylabones™

Digging

Digging is a natural and instinctual behavior for dogs. It is important to understand and identify the underlying reasons why a dog digs. Some dogs dig cooling pits to lie in, others bury things. Some dig after vermin or as a means of escaping the yard, or because they are just plain bored. Many dogs dig because digging is simply an enjoyable pastime. A number of things can be done to channel and correct your dog's digging. First, it is important to realize you can't train a dog you are not with. Most people who experience digging problems leave their dogs outdoors unsupervised. Keep it confined in a safe area when you cannot supervise and teach. A key factor to solving any dog problem is prevention.

First, make sure your dog is vigorously exercised and receives ample daily attention. If you must keep your dog outside make sure the yard is adequately shaded. If your dog digs to bury bones refer to the advice on food possessiveness later in this chapter. Dogs sometimes dig under the fence to satisfy their urge to reproduce. Spay/neuter surgery will curtail this problem. If the dog is already involved in digging and the natural instinct and pleasures of digging have been strongly reinforced and rewarded, it may be necessary to create a digging pit.

A digging pit is a chosen place where a dog is encouraged to dig. The owner may bury some interesting toys in the pit while the dog watches. The dog is then enthusiastically encouraged to dig them up and is praised. The dog should be confined to the well-stocked digging area when the owner is not present. This will encourage the habit of digging in the right area.

The owner must spend time in the yard watching the dog closely. The dog must be immediately corrected. Use a verbal command the instant the dog begins inappropriate digging: **GO TO YOUR PIT**. Reward your dog if it begins digging in the assigned area.

Chicken wire buried at an angle or a strong piece of plywood driven vertically two feet into the ground may discourage digging to escape.

Remember the dog's social and exercise needs. Are they being met? If not, they may contribute to problem digging and misbehavior. Digging is a natural behavior for a dog. Beware of taking a corrective approach only. A dog must be taught acceptable behavior. If in doubt about what to do, consult a professional trainer or behaviorist.

Excessive Barking

Barking to a dog is like singing to a canary or talking to a human — a natural, normal behavior. This normal behavior may occur at inappropriate times or become too excessive and tiresome if not controlled by the owner. Barking is a way of communicating a message. It is usually triggered by excitement. Some dogs are more prone to excessive barking than others. This may be due to genetics, poor direction from the owner, lack of exercise or boredom.

Some of the most common reasons for barking are:

- Barking for attention and lack of social contact.
- Barking out of boredom or need.
- Barking out of stress, fear or frustration.
- Barking because of strong territorial instincts.
- Barking to assert dominance.
- Barking to control movement.

Barking can be controlled. Many owners make the mistake of trying to soothe the dog by patting and stroking during barking. Unknowingly, they are rewarding the dog for barking, and, in effect, training the dog to bark. Try to understand what is causing your dog to bark. Do you stroke the dog in a soothing manner during barking? Are you aware of the dog's breed characteristics and tendencies to bark? Do you satisfy a dog's social instincts by making him a part of the family? Do you provide a proper diet, quality time and training? Early morning exercise will expend and vent excess energy and keep the dog more content during the day. Do you provide mental stimulation as well as physical? Do you teach your dog tricks and work on obedience commands? Do you punish your dog for barking without teaching him appropriate barking?

In order to keep the peace with your neighbors and prevent the relinquishment of your dog, you must address the problem. When you are not there bring your dog inside. Keep your dog from viewing activity on the street. When you are there to supervise, teach the dog to distinguish between appropriate and inappropriate barking. This may be accomplished by introducing the dog to regular service people, the mail person, utility workers, gardeners and meter readers. Make sure you reward the dog for not barking. Teach your dog the meaning of the word "quiet" by putting the barking on cue. Use the command **QUIET** or **CEASE.**

Most dogs bark when a doorbell rings. You may take advantage of this by setting up a training situation. You'll need an assistant. Assistant quietly goes to your front door. You say: **ROVER, SPEAK**! This is the cue for assistant to ring bell. Dog barks, you say **GOOOOD SPEAK, ROVER, GOOOD SPEAK**! Repeat several times. Now while the dog is barking say **OK** now, **ROVER, QUIET**. (Say this in a firm tone while gently cupping dog's muzzle closed). Reward for ceased barking. **GOOOOD QUIET, ROVER**! If the dog barks, verbally reprimand immediately. If the dog continues, put the dog in a prolonged down/stay. Repeat the process until you are successful. Try to work up to 15 to 20 minutes of quiet or longer. Always remember to reward the dog for being quiet. Be consistent! Practice these exercises while spending time in the yard with your dog. If a person walks by and the dog barks, say **GOOD SPEAK**. Then **ROVER, QUIET**. Barking is something that can be controlled. If barking is a constant problem, you may need to work with a professional behaviorist.

Jumping Up

Jumping by dogs is a natural instinctive behavior. When dogs jump on people, they are trying to greet and get near the face of their pack members, which is a dog's way of showing affection. Jumping up, although natural, is unacceptable to humans and can be dangerous. There is nothing more annoying to some people than to be bounded on by an enthusiastic pooch, regardless of its size. Jumping is usually exhibited when a dog first meets people.

The best way to stop your dog from jumping is to teach him to sit and stay. Then get down to the dog's level to greet him. There are dozens of things a dog cannot do while sitting and staying. Jumping is one of them. Avoid overexciting your dog when a guest arrives.

Ask friends to participate in a simulated training session. Have a friend come to the door. Place your dog in a sit/stay. After a period of time your dog should calm down and assume a normal manner. Be consistent. Don't let the dog jump up on you and then correct the dog if it jumps up on your friends. Anticipate jumping situations. Have a leash available at all times and use it for control. Another effective method is to turn your back on the dog when he jumps. Pay no attention to him until he settles down. Then greet him.

Please don't kick, knee or step on the feet of your dog as some so-called experts recommend. You could damage your dog and all because, in his way, he wanted to affectionately greet you.

Excitement/Submissive Urination

Dogs that urinate when greeting are exhibiting submissive or over-excited behavior. Punishing or drawing attention to the behavior will make it worse. The way of greeting and interacting with the dog must be changed. There are several ways in which owners can greet submissive dogs and minimize the probability of eliciting submissive urination.

For instance, the owner can squat down while keeping the upper body straight. Avoid direct eye contact, vigorous petting and speaking in a high or excited voice. Redirecting the pup's attention by tossing a toy or piece of food before greeting will also help. The owner may also teach the pup to sit/stay for greetings and practice in easy situations. Handling the problem in the right way should eliminate the problem.

Possessiveness

It is not unusual for a dog to growl or even bite when someone approaches his food dish or prized possession. This is a natural response that, in the wild, ensures survival, but in homes is inappropriate and dangerous. Punishment is not an effective approach and may make matters worse. Teach pups that the presence of people around his food dish is something very positive.

Start announcing chow time by shaking the food bag. Ask your dog to sit and put down his empty bowl. Drop two or three pieces of kibble into the bowl. After the pup eats them repeat the procedure three or four times. Next, drop more kibble into the bowl. While the pup is eating, offer him a small piece of chicken with your hand next to his bowl. Repeat. Now, put more kibble in the dish and, while the pup is eating, pick up the bowl, add a piece of chicken, give it back to him. Now, while the pup is eating, gently pet him and offer more desirable treats.

Children should also use this exercise after the dog readily accepts the food from adults without signs of aggression. By practicing this exercise, your dog will learn that your hands come to give, not to take away. A trust will develop.

Make sure your pup will relinquish objects to you. Start by pressing firmly but gently at the dog's muzzle directly behind the two canine teeth. The pressure will cause the dog to open his mouth. Now, while he is holding a favorite chew toy press at the muzzle and say **OUT** or **GIVE**. When the dog relinquishes the article, praise and give it back to him. Repeat the procedure several times with many different objects, always ending the session with the dog keeping the article.

These exercises are to prevent aggression. If you own a dog that is already exhibiting threatening behavior, do not attempt this exercise on your own. Seek the help of a qualified behaviorist.

Aggression

There are two types of aggressive behavior: toward other dogs and toward people. Both types can be avoided if your dog is properly socialized and forms positive associations with other dogs and people at an early age.

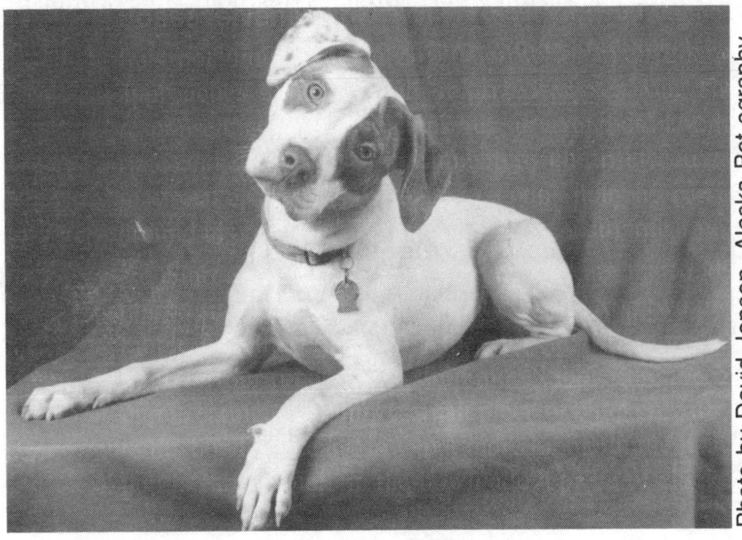

Photo by David Jensen, Alaska Pet-ography

Are You a Harsh Owner?

A common mistake people make is to be too harsh. This can lead to aggressive behavior in your dog. To find out how you interact with your dog answer the following:

- I tie my dog up in the back yard.
- I roughhouse by pushing my dog away so it will lunge back.
- I smack my dog around the face during rough play.
- I wrestle with my dog.
- I push my dog off things or trip it for fun.
- I have to get tough to calm my dog down after play.
- My dog never knows when to quit when I play with it.
- I have gotten angry while playing with my dog.
- I have got hurt when playing with my dog.
- Sometimes I do not respect my dog.
- I have to yell at it to get its attention.
- It only seems to listen or obey when I hit it.
- I have locked my dog up to punish it.
- I have taken things away from my dog as punishment.
- I have made my dog go without meals to teach it a lesson.
- I have punished my dog before leaving home so it will obey while I am gone.
- I have used bitter tasting substances to punish my dog.
- I have used electric shock to punish my dog.
- I have kept my dog outside in extreme weather.

Yes answers indicate a harsh attitude toward your dog.

Aggression Toward Other Dogs

Dogs fight with other dogs mainly because they are not socialized properly, they are not spayed/neutered and they are not receiving proper signals from their owners that indicate this behavior to be unacceptable. Males are involved in the majority of dog fights. They fight over territory, social hierarchy or a female in heat.

The best advice is to prevent fights before they start. Form positive associations with other dogs at an early age. Allow dogs to greet using a loose leash. By restricting the leash the dogs are unable to greet naturally and you give the message to the dog that you are suspicious of the situation. If you witness aggressive barking or lunging, correct your dog and let him know this is unacceptable. Keep dogs separated.

Never hit, punish or treat your dog harshly. Harsh treatment can encourage aggression. If your dog appears agitated by the presence of another dog, never pick up the dog or soothe or stroke your dog. If you do, you're telling the dog you condone his behavior and the behavior will be repeated. Try to act nonchalant. If a dog senses you are threatened, it will encourage and heighten his agitation.

Remember to reinforce positive behavior with happy voice tones when the dog has a good encounter. If you recognize the onset of agitation, distract your dog's attention by using obedience commands or keep a food treat handy and lure the dog's attention away from the other dog. Spaying or neutering in most cases is an effective way to prevent aggression. Never chain a dog in the back yard.

If dogs are fighting, you must make sure you don't endanger yourself. There is no sure, safe way to control the situation. Try throwing water on the dogs, if available. Try using voice control. It is very risky to try to pull the dogs apart. After the fight, seek veterinary attention for your dog.

Aggression Toward People

This is a very serious and complicated problem that should be properly addressed by an experienced behaviorist or trainer. Ask your veterinarian for a recommendation. To prevent aggression make sure your dog is obedience trained, never play tug of war, wrestle or bring your hands to the dog's head as a playful gesture. Socialize your dog at an early age.

How You Might Avoid Being Bitten by a Dog

When dogs might bite

- When they feel threatened or afraid
- When they are protecting their territory, food, toys, family or pups
- When they are startled, like being awakened suddenly
- When they get excited, even in play
- When they don't know you
- When their chase response is triggered
- When they have been bred or trained to be aggressive
- When they are in pain or irritated

Body language of a dog that may bite

- The dog will stand stiff and still, with his hair (hackles) up
- The dog may stare at you
- The dog may hold his tail stiff and up in the air and may wag it back and forth very fast
- The dog may growl, snarl, show teeth or bark strongly

What you can do

- Stand very still and try to be calm; DON'T SCREAM AND RUN
- Don't stare directly at the dog, but be aware of it
- Don't make any sudden moves
- Try to stay until the dog leaves; if it doesn't — very slowly back away
- If the dog comes up to sniff you, don't resist
- If you say anything, speak calmly and firmly
- Plan, in case of attack, to buffer a bite with a purse, jacket or other object
- Climb a tree or jump on a car hood
- If you fall or are knocked down, curl into a ball with your arms and hands over your head and neck; try not to scream or roll around
- If you get bitten, report all bites to police or animal control, seek treatment and remember to give a description to the authorities so they can find the animal and determine if the dog has rabies

The Home Alone Dog

Provide early-morning and after-work regular exercise. Provide a safe confinement area for your dog when you are gone. Make sure the area is free from hazards. Use a safe room or a dog run with shade. Use a baby gate or a portable dog pen to engineer an area inside your home. This will prevent problems from occurring and keep the dog safe.

Make your pet feel comfortable by providing a blanket, soft music, safe chew toys and a bowl of water. Don't leave food out all day. Feed at regular times for twenty minutes only. Break up the day by using pet sitters, doggie day care, neighborhood friends or a responsible neighborhood boy or girl you can trust to let the dog out, take it for a walk and play with it, or, if you can make it home for lunch all the better. Don't make a big fuss over your departures and arrivals. Establish a routine. Provide the dog with quality time when you are home.

Use positive obedience training to build your dog's confidence and provide mental stimulation. As a general rule, crates should not be used for more than 3 to 4 hours. The exception is overnight sleeping, at which time the dog should be let out in the middle of the night if needed until 6 months of age. Dogs are social animals and may benefit from the company of another dog.

Outside Dogs and Backyard Boredom

Dogs are pack animals and happiest living with the companionship of their human pack family. Dogs need interaction and affection from their owners. That's why they make such great pets. Surveys reveal 70% of dog owners allow their dogs indoors. When dogs are relegated to the back yard, many behavior problems can develop.

Barking, whining and destructive behaviors like chewing and digging are all cries for help. What the dog is saying is: I need your attention, I want to be around you, just show me how to behave. It only takes a short time to work out any problems associated with keeping the dog indoors. A good training program can help you and your dog make the adjustment and help you deal successfully with any problem. If you absolutely must keep your dog outdoors during the day consider bringing the dog indoors at night and at times when the family is present. Most dogs that live indoors will alert you to the presence of a stranger on your property. Consider a second dog for company if you absolutely must keep your dog outside.

Never chain your dog in the back yard. Dogs are not meant to be confined in this manner and will become ill-tempered.

Game Playing

Games not only provide exercise, but also give your dog the opportunity to use his mental capabilities. Games can strengthen your communication and reinforce the human/dog bond.

They can be as simple as throwing a stick to be retrieved or as advanced as sending your dog through an agility course. Games should always be controlled, initiated and ended by you. When the game is over, remove the object or toy. Games can be used as a reward and to motivate in training. Here are a few games:

Photo by Sumner Fowler, Marin Humane Society

- Fetch or Retrieve. Teach your dog to retrieve by using the cardboard roll that comes on the inside of toilet paper. Rap duct tape around the tube to keep it sturdy. Place treats inside then seal the ends with two pieces of a used sponge. Start the session by showing the roll to your dog. Slightly tease him with the object to promote interest. Throw the object a short distance. The dog should retrieve the roll. When he successfully brings the roll back to you and releases it, open one of the ends and give him a treat. Repeat.
- Hide and Seek. Place your dog in a sit/stay. Find a hiding place and command your dog to **Find.**
- Find it. Show your dog the item, then hide it and give him the command to **Find It.**
- Teach your dog tricks like roll over, bow, beg, play dead, bang or pray.
- Agility and obstacle courses. Call a local club.

Don't play tug of war, wrestle or pin your dog, push your dog away, or continually bring your hands up to the dog's muzzle. These games encourage aggression.

Make sure that after you play, your dog has the chance to relieve himself.

Dog Behaviorists

Dog behaviorists are people who study the way dogs act and react to their environment by taking into account the dog's evolutionary development. Behaviorists try to convey in everyday language why dogs behave a certain way in certain situations. They use this knowledge to modify negative behaviors and to help integrate the dog into the human world in which it lives.

If You Experience Problems

If you experience problems that you have been unsuccessful in solving consult with your adoption agency. They may have someone on staff to assist you. If not, ask your veterinarian for a referral to a reputable behaviorist or trainer. Many of these problems can be successfully modified with minor adjustments.

Canine Wellness

Healthy Signs

Skin should be smooth, supple and free of scales, scabs, growths or areas of redness.

Coat should be glossy and pliable, without dandruff or areas of baldness. There should be no external parasites or mats.

Eyes should be bright and shiny, free from excessive watering or discharge.

Ears should be light pink, clean with a small trace of wax.

Nose is usually cold and moist. However, a warm nose does not mean a sick dog.

Temperature is normally 100 to 102.5 degrees (average 101.5).

Gums should appear pink, firm and may have black or gray pigment.

Teeth should be clean and free of tartar. Breath should be odor free.

Pulse is 70 to 130 beats per minute at rest.

Stools should be firm, tan or brown and free of parasites.

Exercise

Regular exercise is one of the most important things you can do for the mental, emotional and physical health of your dog. A big benefit of owning a dog is that a dog encourages walks and/or runs that are good for both owner and dog.

Photo by Sumner Fowler, Marin Humane Society

As a general rule, a twenty- to thirty-minute walk twice a day, along with an occasional hard run is sufficient. Regularly scheduled exercise will help vent a lot of energy that, if pent up for long, can manifest itself in problem behaviors. Exercise can eliminate the desire to roam and escape. The amount of exercise depends on the dog's age and size. Don't vigorously exercise your dog one hour before or one hour after meals, especially if your dog is prone to bloat. Lack of exercise will eventually make your dog lethargic, listless and prone to obesity.

Walking Dogs can benefit most from morning sessions because this is the time when they are most energetic. Unfettered male dogs will want to mark their territory. As dogs grow older they may become stiff in joints. Be sympathetic, adjust your walk length and try to introduce other games to keep your old pal stimulated. Watch out for hot pavement. It may burn your dog's paw pads. Consult your veterinarian about medication to relieve your dog's arthritic discomfort.

Running Before you begin running with your dog consider his breed, age and health condition. Make sure your dog is safe and on a leash. Start slowly and protect your dog's feet. Be aware of extreme weather conditions. Don't overdo it. Make sure you provide plenty of water after the run, watch for injury and make sure you take plastic bags to clean up any droppings.

Retrieving Teach your dog to retrieve. If you throw a ball, your dog will search, run after it, and bring it back with great pleasure and receive a lot of exercise. Start at an early age and make it exciting. Praise and reward your dog when he successfully retrieves. Make coming to you pleasurable. Don't throw hard objects that may crack your dog's teeth.

Hiking When you want to enjoy the great outdoors with your dog follow these tips:

Make sure your dog is up to date on its vaccinations (Lyme, Parvo, rabies, distemper, heartworm prevention) and is in good health. Consult with your veterinarian. Train your dog with walks over a period of weeks and months that increase in distance and ultimately equal the length of the planned hike.

Check in advance to see if dogs are allowed on the trail. Some parks ban dogs, others require leashed dogs, and others will allow dogs to be off leash.

Bring doggie snacks. Consider a dog pack, but remember your dog is not a pack mule. Use a leash, preferably a retractable one. Dogs can spot a wild animal and be gone in a split second, especially the hunting and hound breeds. Unleashed dogs can also damage sensitive plant life.

Make sure your dog has ID tags and they are securely fastened before you leave for your hike. Bring plenty of water and a plastic bowl and don't let your pet drink stagnant water. They are susceptible to the same diseases that people are. Watch out for rushing water and make sure your dog is leashed when crossing streams.

Don't let your dog approach other hikers unless the other hikers initiate the approach. Don't forget a first-aid kit that includes gauze pads, gauze, adhesive tape, disinfectant and tweezers. Check your dog for ticks and remove immediately with tweezers (be sure you get the head).

Keep your dog from overheating. Stop and rest in a shady area. If you see your dog excessively panting, cool by giving water both internally and externally. Every year many dogs die from overheating on extended outings. Consider apparel for you and your dog that glows in the dark and can be easily identified by hunters, such as a bright orange vest.

Agility This sport is a lot of fun. It is like a visit to a doggy amusement park that provides an outlet for energy and is a great way to spend free time with your companion. Agility works a dog physically and mentally. In this sport, dogs traverse a maze of obstacles and compete for speed and accuracy. Dogs jump through tires, zip through tunnels, scale a 6-foot-tall A-frame, walk a narrow dog walk, negotiate a seesaw, zigzag through poles and soar over a variety of hurdles. Dogs can participate early. They learn to improve their skill with practice. Call your local agility club to find out how you can get started.

Dog Food & Nutrition

The following are a few basic rules of nutrition:

Choose the highest-quality food you can afford. Quality ingredients in the food cost the manufacturer more and therefore cost you more, but the food is easily digested and has a higher percentage of nutrients that are absorbed in the dog's system. Lesser-quality food has more indigestible fillers, which result in greater stool volume. Quality food is more concentrated. You don't have to feed as much as you would a cheaper dog food to meet your dog's daily nutritional requirements. In the long run, the cost per serving may be less.

There are three types of commercial dog food: dry, semi-moist and canned.

Dry This type of food has only 10% to 20% water. The food is combined and cooked under high pressure. Tiny cubes are formed when cooked food is pressed through tiny openings in the machine. After it dries, the food is treated with a pleasing taste and preserved. It becomes crunchy in texture. Dry food is favored for dental hygiene.

Semi-moist This type of food contains 25% to 30% water. It comes shaped like a giant sausage. You can slice patties similar to hamburgers.

Canned This type of food has approximately 75% water content. It comes in different combinations of meat, meat by-products and cereals. Dogs favor the taste of canned food. Some people will mix canned with dry to improve palatability.

All commercial dog foods are formulated to contain the basic building blocks of canine nutrition: protein, fat, carbohydrates, vitamins and minerals. They must exist in proper balance proportioned for the life stage and activity level of your dog. Calcium/phosphorus ratio levels must be maintained within a range of 1.2% calcium to 1% phosphorus, no more, no less. Zinc is an important mineral that must be included in diets. You can do considerable harm by feeding homemade diets that are nutritionally incomplete. *Dogs, unlike people, do not need variety in their diets.*

High cost and high quality may not be one and the same. You must familiarize yourself with labels in order to determine the quality of the food. Labels must list the ingredients in descending order by weight, along with a guaranteed analysis of the product's protein, fat, fiber and moisture content. You should also look for a claim about its nutritional value for a particular life stage. If manufacturers claim high protein on the label, know the source. The most readily digestible protein for a dog is the white of an egg, which is given a biological value rating of 1 by nutritionists, followed by muscle meats, .90; beef, .84; fish, .75; soy, .75; rice, .72; oats, .66; yeast, .63; wheat, .60; and corn, .54. The cost per pound would fall in the same order. Look on the label to determine from what source the protein is derived. Too many vague terms on the labels are still used and allowed by the government, which makes it difficult to compare food quality. In the final analysis, you need to choose a dog food manufacturer that you can trust.

Do not feed table scraps, but if you can't resist those pleading eyes, limit table scraps to no more than 10% to 15% of the diet.

Don't give your dog chocolate! It can be deadly. Feed the amount of food necessary to maintain the dog's proper weight and health. Obesity is the number one health problem for dogs. Don't overfeed!

The Association of American Feed Control Officials (AAFCO) has developed protocols for testing dog food based on controlled feedings. To find if your food has met their approval call: 1-800-851-0769.

Seek the advice of your veterinarian, especially if your dog has dry skin or allergies. They recommend and sell special diets formulated for specific conditions.

Food Formulated for Age

Commercial dog foods are formulated for your dog's age. The following is an example of the time it takes for your dog to mature.

Size	Weight	Age at Maturity
Toys	up to 15 lbs.	6 months
Small	15-35 lbs.	9 months
Medium	35-55 lbs.	10-15 months
Large	55-100 lbs.	18-20 months
Giant	100-175 lbs.	22 months

Vitamins for Dogs

Never supplement your dog's diet before consulting your veterinarian. Most commercial dog foods are sound nutritionally. It could be dangerous to supplement vitamins without the advice of a knowledgeable professional who is aware of your pet's individual health status. Excessive amounts of vitamins are toxic, and minerals like calcium and phosphorus must be kept in the correct balance.

Obesity Test

To determine if your dog is obese, place your hands on its rib cage. You should be able to feel the ribs by gentle pressure. If you cannot, your dog is overweight. Feeding your dog too much is as bad as not feeding your dog enough. Overweight dogs can develop many problems and their lives can be shortened.

Grooming

Every dog should be groomed thoroughly and regularly. Regular grooming is essential to good health and will help you bond with your dog. Long-haired dogs require more grooming. The grooming routine includes attention to the coat, teeth, nails, eyes and ears. The time and effort varies depending on your breed. It is a good opportunity to check for any bumps, dry skin, external parasites, foxtails and burrs. Early detection can be a lifesaver. If any problems exist you should proceed to your veterinarian for treatment. It's up to you to be your dog's best friend by looking after his physical needs on a regular basis.

Photo by Sumner Fowler, Marin Humane Society

Coat All dogs should be brushed once a day. Not only will your dog be neat and clean, but it will feel better as well. Dogs love it.

First, feel your dog all over for any foreign objects and remove them carefully. Using a brush recommended for your breed, hold the hair up a small section at a time and brush downward in short, brisk strokes. When you have done the entire body this way, begin again at the head and use long sweeping strokes to brush in the direction the hair grows to smooth the coat. Make sure you don't pull or hurt the skin.

Talk to your dog in a reassuring tone while you are grooming. Be firm, not harsh if he tries to resist. Soon he will understand that you are not going to hurt him. He will learn to enjoy the sessions. Professional groomers should be used periodically. Consult with a professional groomer for the kind of grooming equipment you will need for your dog.

Bathing Frequent baths remove natural oils and are not good for dogs. Twice a month baths are recommended, with an occasional extra bath depending on need. Only use a shampoo formulated for dogs.

Pads and Nails Your dog's feet require special attention. Always check between the dog's toes for dirt and foreign objects and possible hair mats. Nails should be trimmed every other week to clear the floor. Purchase a specially designed nail trimmer or rasp at your pet store. Don't use scissors. Ask your groomer or veterinarian to show you how. A dog's nails are sensitive. They should not be clipped too high at first. This would cause the quick, which is a vein running through the nail, to bleed. The length of this vein varies. The best approach is to take a little off the tip frequently. This will cause the quick to recede and allow you to cut the nail shorter each time.

Ears At least once a week dirt, dust, and earwax should be removed from the ears using a cotton swab. Proceed gently, and do not probe deeply. Cut any excessive hair. Clean only the outer ear. The inner ear should be cleaned and earwax removed by a professional. If your dog scratches behind the ears a lot, or keeps shaking its head violently, or both, it may have an infection. Do not try to clean out an infected ear; seek the help of your veterinarian.

Eyes Make sure hairs do not rub against the eyeball, and any discharge is removed. If there is any inflammation, reddening, tearing or excessive blinking, your veterinarian should be consulted.

Teeth Dogs develop plaque and tartar just as people do. Start at an early age and get your dog accustomed to tooth brushing. You should clean your dog's teeth twice a week. Use a regular toothbrush and toothpaste formulated for dogs. Older, hardened deposits should be removed by your veterinarian.

How to Choose a Groomer

There are no special government licenses or requirements to become a groomer. It is important you know as much as possible about the person to whom you are about to entrust your dog. How long have they been grooming? How did they learn to groom?

Ask your veterinarian for references. Visit the grooming shop before you make your first appointment. Is the shop clean and sanitized? How are the other dogs being treated? Will your dog be in contact with other animals? Is your groomer certified by a national or local grooming association? What shampoo is being used on your pet? What flea-killing agent? What drying techniques? When practiced properly, grooming should be an enjoyable experience. Look for signs of mishandling when you pick up your dog. Is your dog frightened or timid? Notice how your dog reacts toward the groomer. When you pick up your dog you should expect nails trimmed, ear hair removed, ears swabbed clean, tummy and pads shaved, coat trimmed according to breed standard, correct shampoo for skin type, and a warning about any noticeable problems. The National Dog Groomers Association of America sets standards and service guidelines for its members and conducts certification programs.

When you pick up your pet check its ID tag. Give your dog praise and attention when you pick it up. This helps create a positive association with the grooming experience.

First-Aid Kit

You may need these items:

- Rectal thermometer (Normal temperature is 100.8 to 102.5)
- Petroleum jelly
- Hydrogen peroxide for cuts and wounds and to induce vomiting
- Sterile gauze pad and adhesive tape (1 inch wide) and cotton balls
- A triple antibiotic ointment for surface wounds
- A flat board or cardboard box, blanket or towel to use as a stretcher, if needed
- Toothbrush and dog toothpaste
- Blunt-tip scissors
- Rounded-tip tweezers

Summer Cautions

Hot days Make sure your dog has plenty of fresh water, shade and air. Your dog may eat a little less than usual. Check your pets regularly for fleas. Avoid hot cars. Watch out for garden pesticides.

Hot cars Make sure you don't leave your pet in a car during the hot summer months. Temperatures can heat up within a few minutes to unbearable and dangerous levels. If you have to take your pet, park in the shade and provide a constant air supply. The best advice is to *leave your dog at home!*

Heatstroke Dogs are susceptible to heatstroke. Be mindful of shade and water and excessive activity during hot weather. Take long dog walks early in the morning or early in the evening. If you think your dog has heat exhaustion, immediately apply cool water with a garden hose and proceed to a veterinarian. When a dog's rectal temperature is 104 or more, the dog is in serious trouble.

Swimming Most dogs love to swim, but don't assume your dog knows how. Go into the water with a stick or ball and call your dog. Never frighten your dog or throw him in. Don't let him overdo. Be careful of strong tides and access to the beach. Many dogs have drowned because they couldn't climb up the embankment or concrete wall of the swimming pool. If you have a pool, teach the dog how to use the steps. Be aware drinking ocean water can cause diarrhea. Stagnant lakes and ponds may contain harmful bacteria and parasites.

Snakebite Symptoms include swelling, labored breathing, glazed eyes and drooling. Proceed to veterinarian while keeping the dog warm, calm and inactive.

Bee stings Dogs are prone to investigate bees. Stings produce pain and swelling. A dog that has a severe reaction needs veterinary attention. An ice cube over the sting will ease the pain and swelling. Seek the advice of your veterinarian.

Disaster Preparedness and Your Dog

Take a few minutes and make preparations that could save the life of your best friend:

- It is vitally important to always keep ID tags on your pet as a primary means of reuniting with your dog in case it ever becomes lost. In addition to your name and number, use a contact number for a person that is out of your area. Dogs are likely to run away in an emergency. In addition, you should also consider a microchip implant. The microchip is safely imbedded under the skin. Many shelters are using this technology as a means of identifying stray dogs.
- Two weeks' supply of canned and dry pet food
- Two weeks' supply of bottled water
- Flashlights, batteries, candles and radio
- Can opener
- Heavy blanket

- Set of bowls
- Crate
- Two leashes per dog
- First-aid kit and medications
- Health and vaccination records
- Photo, in case your dog gets lost
- Secure all bookcases and cabinets to the wall if you live in danger of earthquake damage.
- Ask a neighbor, in advance, to care for your dog in the event you are away and can't get home when disaster strikes.
- Have a plan for boarding. Know hotels that accept pets. Line up a reputable kennel. Red Cross shelters do not accept animals inside their buildings.
- Obtain a pet notice sticker from your local fire department. This will alert emergency personnel that a pet(s) lives in your house.
- Keep some emergency supplies in your car.

Photo by Sumner Fowler, Marin Humane Society

Life Expectancy

The length and quality of your dog's life will depend on genetics, nutrition and care. You can't control genetics, but you can have an influence on nutrition and care.

Pets age at a much more rapid pace than people. Small and medium dogs age fifteen human years their first year then nine years the next year and four years every year from two on. A seven-year-old dog would be 44. Large and giant breeds age 12 years the first human year and 7 years thereafter. A 5-year-old dog would be 40 in human years.

Care of the Senior Dog

About 12% of the dog population is over 10. These special friends need thoughtful care in order to make their remaining time comfortable. Your veterinarian should be consulted as to the best care to prolong the quality of life for your dog. Pay close attention to feeding and nutrition, grooming and preventive care.

Activity levels and metabolism rates slow, reducing the amount of calories required. Your dog may need a special diet formulated for older dogs. If you don't make the adjustment, your dog can become overweight, hastening illness. Obesity is the greatest danger to the dog's well-being. It is the direct cause of many illnesses and without question, reduces the life span of your pet.

There is considerable debate over the amount of protein that a senior dog should consume. Some experts say the amount of protein should be reduced; others say it should remain the same. For best direction consult with your veterinarian. Because older dogs eat less, their diet should be of high quality to supply the necessary daily nutrients. Because digestion and absorption take longer, try feeding smaller portions more often, but no more than their daily caloric requirement.

Senior dogs should have regular examinations at least once yearly and perhaps more depending on overall health. Vaccinations should be up-to-date. Ideal weight should be maintained. Moderate exercise helps to fight obesity and keep the joints supple. Regular walks keep the older dog fit and help relieve boredom.

Older dogs adjust poorly to physical and emotional stress. They love routine. Special care should be exercised to prevent exposure to extremes in weather and to provide a shelter away from rain, cold and drafts.

Make sure your dog's teeth are clean and free of tartar to prevent bad breath, gingivitis and periodontic disease. The older dog's coat dries and becomes brittle. Skin tumors are more common. Kidney disease is a common problem. Take your senior dog out more frequently to avoid bladder infection. Bladder "leaking" is not normal even in older dogs and should be reported to your veterinarian. Place papers by the door at night for the dog's convenience.

Frequent brushings, combined with regular bathing with a specially-formulated shampoo recommended by your veterinarian is advised. Toenails need to be trimmed more often. When wet, your dog should be towel-dried thoroughly and kept in a warm room. Try to keep the aged dog interested and happy. A younger dog may help.

Euthanasia

When life becomes difficult and ceases to be enjoyable, when your dog is old, terminally ill, sick and suffers from a painful condition for which there is no hope of betterment, it is time to say good-bye. This is a tough decision, but one of the kindest acts a loving owner can do to relieve the dog of suffering.

Death of a Family Pet

As an integral part of the family, the dog that has died can affect family members emotionally. Intense grief over the loss of a pet is normal and natural for all dog lovers. Unfortunately, there are no social rituals like funerals and wakes that act to support us during these troubled times. A lot of people who don't understand the human/animal bond may find it hard to sympathize. Still, the loss of a pet affects our emotions and usually progresses through several stages. Recognizing them can help people cope with the grief. The stages are:

Denial This is the initial response many owners exhibit when faced with their pet's terminal condition or sudden death.

Anger This can be exhibited by hostility and aggression or can be turned inward, emerging as guilt. You can get angry at your veterinarian or someone else, but you are just relieving frustration at the expense of another. You can also go through a number of *if only's*, i.e., if only I had acted earlier.

Grief This is the stage of true sadness. The pet is gone and only emptiness remains. It is important to have the support of family and friends and to talk about your feelings. It is helpful to recognize that other pet owners have experienced similar feelings and that you are not alone in this feeling of grief.

Resolution All things must pass, even grieving. As time passes, the distress dissolves as the pet owner remembers the good times, not the passing. If you need to tell children, be honest. Make it clear that the pet has lived its life, it was well cared for while with you and now the pet is at peace. Many people have to wait to obtain another dog; others find the answer lies in giving a good home to a dog in need of a good owner. If, at some point, you do get a new dog, try not to compare the new dog with your lost dog. Every dog has its own personality and unique qualities.

Look for a pet-loss support group near you. Call your local shelter.

Rainbow Bridge

Just this side of heaven is a place called Rainbow Bridge.

When an animal dies that has been especially close to someone here, that pet goes to rainbow bridge. There are meadows and hills for all of our special friends so they can run and play together. There is plenty of food and water and sunshine, and our friends are warm and comfortable. All the animals who had been ill and old are restored to health and vigor; those who were hurt or maimed are made whole and strong again, just as we remember them in our dreams of days and times gone by.

The animals are happy and content, except for one small thing: they miss someone very special to them; who had to be left behind.

They all run and play together, but the day comes when one suddenly stops and looks into the distance. The bright eyes are intent; the eager body quivers. Suddenly he begins to break away from the group, flying over the green grass, his legs carrying him faster and faster. YOU have been spotted, and when you and your special friend finally meet, you cling together in joyous reunion, never to be parted again. The happy kisses rain upon your face; your hands again caress the beloved head, and you look once more into the trusting eyes of your pet, so long gone from your life but never absent from your heart.

Then you cross rainbow bridge together.....

—Anonymous

7

Health Care

Veterinarians

A healthy dog is a happy dog. The key person in the health and care of your dog is your veterinarian. Americans spend $4.6 billion a year on veterinary care. Dog owners average 2.5 visits and spend $132 per year at veterinary facilities, according to a 1991 survey by the American Animal Hospital Association.

Photo by Click, the Photo Connection

Regularly scheduled visits will ensure your dog grows into a fit and healthy adult. It is far easier to prevent illness than to cure disease. Your veterinarian will offer advice on general health care and keep your dog on the road to well-being. Regular visits will alert you to the need for any vaccines, make sure the dog is free of parasites (both internal and external), and head off many major problems. The veterinarian will ask you questions to have a good understanding of the dog's activities and determine if there are any abnormal signs. A physical examination will be performed. An accurate diagnosis sometimes requires the use of lab tests, X-rays, and specialized equipment.

A yearly preventive health check will, in the long run, save you money on your dog's veterinary care. More importantly, it will help ensure that your dog will not have to suffer needlessly. Many veterinarians support shelter adoptions by offering a free exam on the initial visit.

Tips on Choosing a Veterinarian

Develop a partnership with a good veterinarian and the staff that includes a complete life plan for total health care. Ask friends and neighbors with pets for referrals. Call several veterinary clinics in your area and arrange a visit without your dog. Look for a veterinarian who will take the time to speak with you and will make the effort to explain any problems in layman's terms. Ask if they are available for telephone consultation. Ask to tour the facility. Look for cleanliness, lack of odor, and a comfortable environment for the patient and owner. If you don't feel comfortable being there, chances are neither will your pet. Is the staff friendly and caring? Do they make you feel comfortable? Are the sick animals isolated from the other animals? What are their hours? Is anyone on duty at night, in case of emergency? Most vets are not open around the clock, but make sure you know whom to call and where to go after hours. All certified veterinarians must have credentials. You should know their credentials and reputation.

You should come away with a confident feeling knowing your pet will be well cared for by a team of competent, compassionate professionals.

Emergencies

Contact your veterinarian *immediately* if your dog exhibits these signs:

- Fainting or convulsions
- Severe lameness
- Cuts, bites or insect stings
- Poisoning (bring the source if possible)
- Bleeding
- Vomiting and/or diarrhea that persists
- Labored breathing or choking
- Overheating (excessive panting)
- Fever
- Persistent cough or sneeze
- Listlessness
- Increased urination or straining to urinate
- Unusual odor or discharge from body openings

Less immediate signs that still need to be checked out:

- A lump or bump on the skin
- Sudden change in behavior like wanting to hide or lethargy
- Loss of appetite
- Lameness that persists without improvement for more than 24 hours
- Persistent scratching or head shaking, particularly if it results in hair loss or reddening of the skin or ears.
- Watery eyes, red eyes or a glassy appearance of the eyes
- Runny nose
- Increased water intake
- Marked weight gain or loss
- Tartar build-up on teeth, red gums or excessive salivation

Important: This list is not all-inclusive. Discuss any irregularity with your veterinarian. You should have a good relationship that includes the ability to feel comfortable in calling your veterinarian with any questions or concerns.

Emergency Animal Hospitals

Your veterinarian should provide you with an after-hours emergency contact or an emergency animal hospital in your area.

First Aid Procedures

First aid should be practiced in an emergency situation before you can reach a veterinarian. First, call your veterinarian and alert him or her to the situation. If you are uncertain about what to do, the veterinarian can advise you on the phone.

Restraint You may find it necessary to muzzle your dog if it is injured. Place a strong bandage or necktie about 3 feet long over the dog's muzzle, tie a simple knot under the chin, cross the ends, and tie them behind the ears.

Emergency transportation Place the dog on a large, firm surface like a plywood board. Large towels or blankets are OK if nothing else is available.

Bleeding Stop the bleeding as quickly as possible. Use a pressure dressing: A gauze pad will normally stop the flow of blood. Wrap it to hold it in place. For severe bleeding in extreme cases, a tourniquet may be necessary. Tourniquets are very dangerous and if not used correctly can cause great damage. Seek the advice of a veterinarian immediately. If used, they should be loosened every ten minutes and should be used only as a last resort. Keep the dog warm and calm. Do not give food or liquids, in case of internal injuries.

Fractures The affected limb is usually held in an unnatural position. Keep the dog as still as possible and transport the dog to your veterinarian using a firm surface. Try to keep the limb supported at all times with a cushion.

Poisoning Seek veterinary care immediately. **Save any of the substance or packaging that the pet may have eaten**. Make sure all household hazardous substances, lawn and garden chemicals, and human medications are safely secured. Be especially cautious of antifreeze, rat poison, snail and gopher bait. One teaspoon of antifreeze can cause kidney damage. Dogs are attracted to the smell and taste of these substances.

If you think your dog has ingested poisons, immediately call your veterinarian and:

National Animal Control Poison Center
University of Illinois
24 hour hot line (fee required)
1-800-548-2423 or 900-680-0000

Vaccines

Don't overlook vaccines. They save millions of dogs' lives yearly. Vaccines prevent such diseases as distemper, parvovirus, parainfluenza, rabies, bordetella, hepatitis, Lyme's and leptospirosis.

The American Veterinary Medical Association recommends that puppies receive a series of vaccinations, beginning at six to eight weeks of age, followed by two more vaccinations three to four weeks apart. Thereafter, renew the protection with booster vaccines each year. The exception to this is the rabies boosters. Laws in many states require up-to-date rabies vaccines starting at four months and a booster vaccine 12 months later. The second rabies vaccination is good for 36 months. Some vaccine schedules will vary depending on the exposure to disease in your area. Consult with your veterinarian to determine a vaccination schedule that's right for your dog.

Nutrition Counseling

Your veterinarian is trained in animal nutrition and can recommend commercial brands of food to suit the nutritional needs of your pet. Some dogs require special "prescription diets" to deal with certain medical situations like obesity, kidney, liver, heart and skin problems among others.

Internal Parasites

Worms can cause serious damage. The most common are:

- Roundworm
- Hookworm
- Whipworm
- Tapeworm

Worms live inside the digestive track of the dog and are seldom seen. A fecal exam performed by your veterinarian is the best way to detect these parasites. A common way an owner notices tapeworms is observing the stool (the tapeworm segments look like white rice grains), but this method is not reliable. Be concerned if you notice your dog rubbing its fanny on the floor or has diarrhea. Don't give your pet over-the-counter medication or remedies for worms without receiving test results. Your veterinarian will prescribe the best and safest medication for your pet.

Heartworm

These parasites are deadly. Every dog owner should be aware of this condition. Heartworm is spread by an infected mosquito that bites a dog. Larvae then burrow into the dog and undergo several changes that lead to the development of worms in the heart. This large thread-like parasite lives in the right ventricle and major arteries of the heart. Ask your veterinarian to recommend a once-a-month tablet to *prevent* heartworm disease.

External Parasites

Fleas, mites and ticks have ruined many dog-owner relationships. It is very important to get a handle on this problem before it's out of control. Ask your veterinarian about a parasite-control program. Fleas spend their life on and off the dog. Treatment of the dog is only partly effective. It is most important to eradicate not only adult fleas, but also emerging flea eggs, larvae and pupae that are in the development stages. You must mount a simultaneous attack on their environment (indoors, outdoors, cars, etc.).

How to Fight Fleas

The signs of fleas include salt-and-pepper-like grains about the size of sand in the coat usually around the dog's back, tail, groin and hindquarters. They are characterized by persistent scratching. If you see one adult flea on your pet, you need to mount your attack.

Every dog owner will have to do battle with the dreaded flea unless he or she lives in a high altitude or year-round cold climate. Fleas are not a sign that you keep an untidy home or that you are a negligent dog owner. They are just a part of dog ownership, especially when the temperature warms.

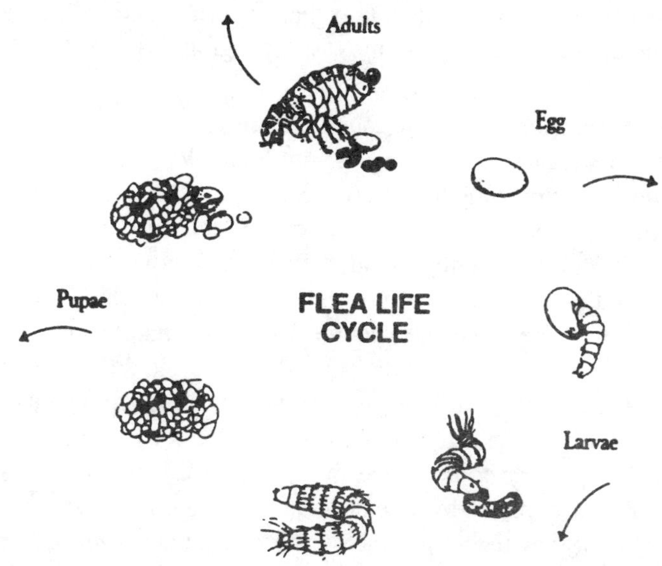

Understanding the life cycle of the flea and adopting a program that effectively treats the dog and its environment is the key to control. Adult fleas comprise only five percent of the total flea population. Their eggs comprise 50%, larvae 35% and pupae 10%. Fleas are most prevalent when the temperature warms. Fleas spend their life on the dog. Treatment of the dog is only partly effective. Flea eggs are laid on the dog and eventually fall to the ground or carpet and hatch within 1-10 days. Insecticides usually do not kill flea eggs. A female flea can lay 40-50 eggs a day for up to 50 days. Within 2 to 12 days, the eggs hatch into larvae. The larvae then spin cocoons. They then hatch into adult fleas in 7 to 14 days. To be successful you must attack not only the flea, but also the flea eggs and the larvae that are in your environment. Otherwise the dog will reinfect itself when new fleas emerge.

Simultaneously mount a three-pronged attack. The main weapons are insecticides such as dips, shampoos especially formulated to kill adult fleas, powders that cling to a dog's coat, sprays to instantly kill adult fleas, bombs to cover large indoor areas and doghouses, and granules used for the outdoor areas or on carpets to penetrate deep into the base.

Treat the dog with a shampoo that is formulated to kill fleas. Treat inside the house with bombs, sprays, granules. Treat the yard with sprays, granules.

The Plan: Start with a thorough cleaning, to eliminate some of the eggs, larvae and fleas lurking in your home. Wash all pet bedding in hot, soapy water. Mop hard floors. Slowly and thoroughly vacuum everywhere — carpets, upholstery, drapes, corners and crevices. Most insecticides will only kill adult fleas. A slow vacuum will take up eggs and larvae. This will prevent them from hatching and reinfesting your home. Seal the vacuum bag immediately in a plastic bag. Spray or use granules in the yard, then treat the dog by taking it to a groomer, veterinarians or give it a bath inside the home using a safe shampoo and flea dip (make sure the dog's eyes and ears are protected). Spray or bomb inside the home, or for long-term results have your house treated by an exterminator company or ask your pet supply store if they recommend a long-term, safe inorganic salt product. Don't forget to treat crates, kennels, runs, bedding, garages and the car. Vacuum often and change the bag!

For most infestations, the cleaning/shampoo/flea comb system is all you will need to achieve flea control.

Choose a product based on the recommendation of your veterinarian. Don't mix dog and cat shampoos.

Insecticides are poisons! Pyrethrums, which are made from chrysanthemums, are claimed to be safe and effective but, like any pesticide, can be toxic if not properly used. Use chemical flea products with caution and only as directed. Don't mix products! Be especially careful with puppies and senior dogs.

Many dogs suffer allergies to flea bites called flea bite dermatitis. Some owners rub on aloe vera for relief. Consult with your veterinarian for an effective course of treatment.

The adult flea harbors a common type of tapeworm. Most dogs will eat a flea while grooming themselves and become infested. To control tapeworms it is important to control fleas.

Check with your veterinarian before applying an insecticide to a dog that has recently received deworming medication.

New Flea Fighter

A new product has been introduced to the United States that prevents flea eggs from maturing. It is an insect-growth regulator called "lufenuron." The trade name is "Program." This product has been safely used for flea control in Canada and Europe for more than five years.

Once taken, lufenuron gets into the bloodstream of the dog and is stored in the fatty layer under the skin. When the flea bites the dog it gets a dose of Program, which prevents it from producing chitin. Any eggs that are laid by adult fleas will never hatch. This product is dispensed by veterinarians and taken once or twice a month, depending on weight. Check with your veterinarian.

Natural Flea Fighters

The following methods are natural flea treatments — not scientifically proven, but *some* owners say they work:

- Avon Skin-So-Soft diluted with water as a spray (repels the fleas).
- Nematodes — microscopic organisms that are released in damp soil. They work to penetrate the flea larvae and pupae and kill them. The soil must be damp in order for them to work.
- Cedar chips.
- Garlic, vinegar or brewer's yeast added to food.
- Fine-toothed flea comb. Collect the fleas in the comb and then drown them in water laced with dish soap, alcohol or flea shampoo. (This can be very effective for short-haired dogs.)
- Herbal flea collars.
- Aloe vera drink for pets.
- Citrus shampoos.

Ticks

These tiny parasites (about the size of a pea) burrow into the skin and feed off the blood supply of your dog. Your dog should be checked after any exposure from walks where ticks dwell. Ticks should be swabbed with alcohol or a special tick solution and then pulled out slowly with tweezers. You must be careful to remove the blood-sucking parasite completely, including the head and biting parts; otherwise, sores and infection may develop.

Be careful not to touch the tick! Many ticks carry Lyme disease that is transmitted to dogs and humans.

Mites

Mites pose a threat to your pet. These tiny organisms live inside your pet's ear or burrow deep into the skin, causing severe itching and inflammation. A microscopic examination is necessary to confirm their presence.

Lyme Disease

Lyme disease is transmitted by ticks. Affected dogs will develop a lameness that may shift from joint to joint. It is possible for humans to contract the disease. Classic symptoms include fatigue, fever and swollen glands in the neck. Consult your veterinarian about the number of incidents in your area and check to see if he or she recommends a vaccination for your dog.

Dermatitis

Dogs get dermatitis from fleas, mites, bacteria, allergies to pollen and chemical irritants. In their attempt to rid themselves of the irritation, they bite and lick themselves. Their sensitive skin becomes infected with bacteria, which causes inflammation and ulceration. Hair loss in the affected area is likely to occur. Be kind to your dog. Consult with your veterinarian as soon as possible. Dermatitis causes pain and discomfort.

Foxtails

In some parts of the country your dog may be exposed to a barbed grass called foxtail. The foxtail is designed to burrow into the earth. This means they can also burrow into your dog's skin, causing great distress and pain. They are difficult for the dog to remove. Protect your dog from the hazards of foxtails by examining it daily, especially between its toes and in its ears. Avoid areas of dry grass and weeds.

Dental Care

It is just as important for you to care for your dog's teeth as you do for your own. Like people, dogs get a build-up of plaque and tartar that must be removed periodically to help prevent major organ damage, tooth loss and unnecessary pain. Periodontic disease is a major health threat. Your veterinarian, who is your dog's dentist, is able to perform this procedure. Prevent tooth decay by brushing your dog's teeth regularly. Get your puppy accustomed to someone opening and examining its mouth. Ask your veterinarian about preventive care.

Pill Medication

The easiest way is to disguise the pill in food. Otherwise, tilt your dog's head upward slightly, then place the pill deep into the dog's throat. Quickly remove your hand and after your dog closes his mouth keep his head elevated and rub or blow on its nose. Usually a dog will lick his nose when he has swallowed the pill. Repeat until successful. Ask your veterinarian to demonstrate. Don't give your dog any medication without your veterinarian's consent.

The American Animal Hospital Association

The AAHA is an international association of more than 12,000 veterinarians who treat companion animals. The association sets standards for quality pet health care practice and evaluates hospitals to ensure compliance. They can be reached by calling 303/986-2800.

The American Veterinary Medical Association

This organization is composed of more than 56,000 veterinarians. Their purpose is to advance the science and art of veterinary medicine and maintain the highest standards of professional competition and conduct. You can contact the organization at 1-800-248-2862.

How Could You?

Kathleen Whiteman

I was just a pup when first we met.
We knew nothing about each other yet.

Those first few weeks, you treated me well,
But, when I had to go out, you'd just yell
That it was up to the kids to let me outside,
When they did not, you paddled my hide!

I did what I could to make our bond strong,
But, being quite young, I did some wrongs
When a month had passed, I heard you say
"Boy do I regret the day!"
A collar of steel you put on me
And chained me to the maple tree.

A shipping crate was my new home,
Into yours again , I'd never roam.
As the years sped by, I longed for you
To talk to me like when I was new!

The kids put food almost in my dish
As I gazed at them and often wished
That I had done something to make you love
me,
Like I do you from this silent tree.

I've guarded the house and barked the alarm
When I thought that something could cause you
harm.
The years have gone by lightening fast,
I lie here reflecting my empty past
I'm feeling my age, I think you can see
That I'm not the young dog that I used to be.

You're standing beside me patting my head,
My heart is breaking, I'm feeling your dread.
Unlocking the chain that bound my lifetime,
I kiss your face for what's the last time.

We go out of the city where the air smells clean,
I really don't think you think your mean.
As you open the door to set me free,
I wish you'd glance back and look at me!
I'd rather be with you although you've strayed
From the one person I've live to obey!

I want it to end by that tall old tree,
Not here, by myself, in the open country!
Don't drive away with tears in your eyes!
Please take me to die 'neath familiar skies!
Forgive me! I'm sorry! I'm scared, can't you
see?

I loved you no matter how bad you'd treat me!
How could you leave me here on this road?
Isn't your guilt a heavy load?
You're driving away in your car alone!
Returning to the only home I've known
Without me! Your dog! Who gave you my years
on the end of a chain. Pleading through tears!

Responsible Dog Ownership

Your Dog and Your Neighbors

All dog owners are responsible for making their dogs good neighbors. Excessive barking, unleashed roaming and unattended excretion are the major problems associated with dogs in urban and suburban areas. Civic leaders are banning more and more places of use for dogs because of irresponsible owners. Be considerate of your neighbor. If your dog barks when left alone outside, consider keeping it inside or, for more severe problems, consult with a dog trainer or behaviorist. Always carry plastic bags on a walk. Leash your dog in public places and always be a responsible, considerate dog owner. Dog care is a lifetime commitment, even when your life style changes. Make sure your pet is a true member of your family by supplying lots of love, care and attention.

Canine Good Citizenship

The American Kennel Club (AKC) promotes canine good citizenship with a certification program that encourages responsible dog ownership. Your dog does not have to be a purebred dog to participate.

Your dog should be trained and conditioned to behave in the home, in public places, and in the presence of other dogs. The testing is an evaluation consisting of ten different activities that a good citizen canine would be expected to be capable of performing.

Photo by Sumner Fowler, Marin Humane Society

Included are allowing a stranger to approach, walking naturally on a loose lead, walking through a crowd, sitting for examination, reacting to a strange dog and reacting to a distraction such as a door suddenly closing or a jogger running closely by the dog.

The evaluator will inspect your dog's grooming appearance and will evaluate the dog's performance on the sit, sit/stay, down and stay in position commands. The last exercise requires the dog to demonstrate good manners when left alone for an extended period of time. Call the AKC at 212/696-8200 to locate an organization in your area that administers the test.

Responsible Dog Owners' Code of Ethics

- Spay/neuter their dog.
- Train their dog.
- Provide daily quality food, fresh water and exercise.
- Provide proper identification worn at all times.
- Observe all state laws and local ordinances.
- Obtain a separate dog license for each dog they own.
- Keep their dog on a leash and prevent it from being a nuisance.
- Keep animal premises sanitary.
- Prevent their dog from biting or intimidating people.
- Pick up and remove waste and place it in a proper receptacle.
- Prevent pregnancy by properly securing their female when in season if the dog is not spayed.
- Consider the peace and quiet of their neighbors and do not allow their dog to bark excessively.
- Never treat an animal cruelly, inhumanely or cause it unnecessary torture or pain.
- When in transit, never transport a dog in an open pickup truck and always ensure the animal's safety.
- Never subject an animal to extreme temperatures by leaving the animal in a vehicle unattended without adequate ventilation.

Artist: Peggy Rushford, Poway, California

These two adorable pets were saved from an abusive situation.

9

Lost and Found

Ten Things to Do If Your Dog Is Lost

The speed and thoroughness with which you react can make the difference in whether you recover your pet. You need to:

1. Organize a search party and call your friends and relatives and direct a search by foot or by car as soon as possible. Station someone in the last place you saw the dog. Leave your scent on an old towel.
2. Ask mail carriers, neighborhood children, neighbors, paper deliverers, utility workers, delivery people, etc., if they have seen a stray dog. Tell a patrolling police officer.
3. Make up cards or fliers with a picture of your dog, description of your dog with any identifiable marks, the dog's name, your name and telephone number where you can be reached in case they spot your pet. Never give your address.
4. Distribute fliers to homes in the area you lost your dog. Put up signs where permitted at intersections, in shopping centers, Laundromats, in vet offices, pet stores and grooming parlors. Make up fliers that include a picture of your pet, both your home and work telephone numbers and a reward offer.
5. Check all local shelters. ***Go in person, daily.*** don't rely on office staff to properly identify your dog. Check the off-limits holding area. Enter your pet information in the lost log, review the found

Photo by Sumner Fowler, Marin Humane Society

log and dead on arrival file. Dogs without ID are usually held a minimum amount of time. Some shelters have a file of private individuals that are holding lost dogs. Bring any information that will prove ownership such as a license, veterinarian records or photo.

6. Offer a reward, especially to neighborhood kids on bikes or skateboards.
7. Check with local veterinarians, emergency clinics, pet shops and groomers and give them a flyer.
8. Advertise in all local newspapers. Watch the found ads and respond to any that might be your dog.
9. Drive or walk around the area at night where you lost your pet. Leave a scent. Call and whistle. Lost pets sometimes hide during the day.

10. Don't give up! Often well-meaning people are afraid to contact local shelters and keep a stray in their home for weeks in hopes of finding the owner.

Unclaimed Pets

Most state laws mandate that a shelter must hold strays for a minimum period of time to give the dog a chance to be claimed. Policy varies from shelter to shelter, but usually dogs that don't have identification are kept for a shorter period than dogs that do. After the time has elapsed, unclaimed pets are evaluated to determine physical health, temperament and overall adoptability. Based on the evaluation, animals are either placed up for adoption or euthanized. The length of time most shelters hold dogs depends on their capacity at the time. If there is a lack of space, many healthy, good-tempered, highly adoptable animals are killed.

Found Pets

If you find a stray dog:

- Ask around the neighborhood. The pet may live close to you. Ask children.
- Call animal control, or take the pet to the shelter yourself. That is where the owner will be looking. Use the "Found" log. Notify all

shelters within a ten-mile radius. Don't wait too long, some owners lose heart after a week of looking.

- You could also place an advertisement in the found section of the newspaper (some papers do not charge) and put up signs in your neighborhood and at intersections.
- Call local veterinarians and groomers.

10

Travel

Airline Travel

Some airlines allow pets to be transported in the passenger cabin if the pet is in an approved carrier and can fit under the seat. Other, larger pets are placed in a pressurized compartment in the underbelly of the plane. Contact the cargo department of the airlines to receive specific information, especially if you are planning a foreign trip where quarantine time and medical certification are necessary. You must make reservations well in advance, preferably on a nonstop early morning flight.

Obtain an airline-approved crate in advance of your flight date. Some airlines and countries require a health certificate that is up-to-date and signed by your vet no later than 10 days prior to flight. Check with your airline for the exact requirements of the country you plan to visit. Prepare the crate. Help your dog become accustomed to the crate well in advance of the flight. Line the bottom of the carrier with a thick layer of newspaper. This will absorb any moisture and insulate against cold temperatures. On the outside tape a piece of paper covered in plastic with your name, address, telephone numbers for both arriving and departing points, your dog's call name, the flight number, destination, and whether you are on board.

Do not feed your adult pet for twelve hours before the flight; allow water up until the time you leave for the airport. Check

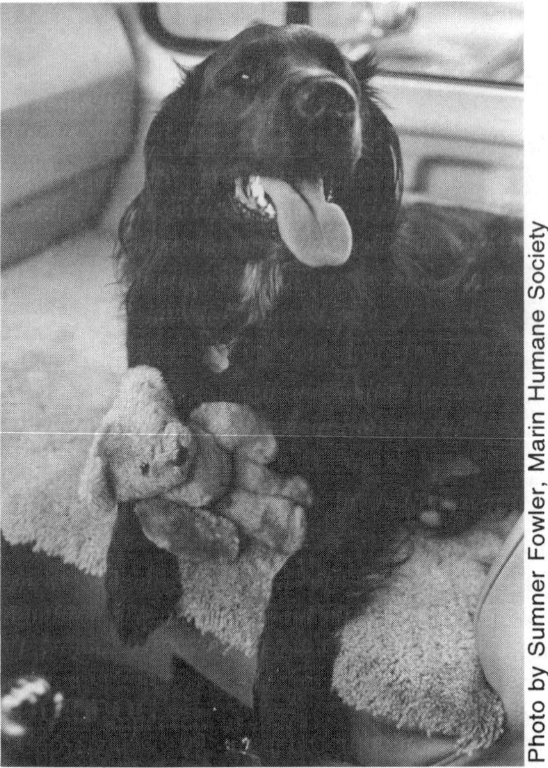
Photo by Sumner Fowler, Marin Humane Society

liability limitations from the airlines. Seek veterinary advice if you are considering tranquilization.

Note: In summer if the temperature is 85 degrees or higher at departure or arrival times airlines by law cannot transport your pet.

Car Travel and Vacations

- Make sure your dog is properly identified. Include information about your destination.
- Give your pet about two hours to digest a meal.
- Make a stop about every two to three hours for exercise, a drink, and for relief.
- Put a leash on your dog before you open the door to exit. A lot of dogs want to jump out of the car the moment the door opens. Make sure you teach your dog the **WAIT** command to prevent it from bolting out the door.

- Crates are safe for motor travel and a nice place for your pet to relax. Use a crate or seat harness for safety.
- If your dog is prone to car sickness, ask a veterinarian about medication. To accustom your dog to car travel, start gradually with short trips. Use lots of reassuring praise. It should eventually grow out of it.

Items for the Canine Travel Kit

- Collar and leash.
- ID tags with home and vacation addresses to be attached to collar.
- Dog food and water bowls.
- The dog's blanket and a couple of old towels.
- A bottle of water and a supply of food.
- Health records and license (if required).
- A first-aid kit with medication for motion sickness and diarrhea, etc.
- Bedding and grooming aids.
- Scooper, plastic bags and paper towels.
- Favorite toy.

Choosing a Boarding Kennel

If you decide you cannot take your dog with you, then choose between a kennel and a dog sitter. You must use care in choosing.

To get into a good kennel, it will be necessary to make advanced reservations, especially during the summer months and around the holidays. The best kennels are usually booked. Visit the kennel. Ask the following questions: How big are the cages? How many dogs occupy each cage? Will your dog be with another strange dog? Will they allow a special reminder of home like a favorite blanket or toy in the cage? Do they have outside runs so your dog does not have to be in the kennel all day? Is there shading? How will your dog be exercised? What about safety procedures like fire alarms, smoke detectors, and overhead sprinklers?

Ask how long they have been in business and how many dogs they board. Make sure the place is well staffed during off hours. Ask if they groom at the facility or if they transport to another location. (There could be a risk of the dogs getting loose if transported.) Ask about veterinary facilities and payment in the event of medical emergency or make arrangements with your vet. Ask for a written confirmation of prices quoted and any extras. Is the kennel clean? Is it air-conditioned in the summer months, heated in the winter? Will your dog have water available at all times? Ask about the food they provide or if you have to bring your own.

A good kennel will request proof of current vaccinations. They are required by law. You may be required to sign a release of liability. Good kennel operators are interested in your dog, they inquire about the dog's medical history, its needs, routines, food and any idiosyncrasies.

11

Diamonds in the Ruff

RANGER: THE RESCUED RESCUER

By Bob Christiansen

Photo by Steven Bloch

Like millions of dogs in shelters across the country, the nameless Newfoundland mix paced anxiously, waiting for someone to rescue him.

Harry Oakes was searching the kennels at the Multnomah County Animal shelter in Troutdale, Oregon. He noticed the big black dog in a kennel off in the corner. Harry began making strange sounds at the dog. The Newfy mix looked puzzled, but didn't retreat. The dog approached Harry and was gently pushed away. The dog returned playfully, his body language said, "Let's be friends." Harry then began to touch the dog from head to toe. The dog did not resist and seemed to enjoy the attention and contact. The man took a long look into the dog's big brown eyes and said to the attendant, "I'll take this one."

Harry runs the Mountain Wilderness Search Dogs (MWSD), International Response Teams in nearby Portland. The nonprofit organization consists of volunteer dog-and-handler teams trained to search for and rescue victims in distress. They respond within 48 hours to calls for help worldwide. When there was an earthquake in the Philippines, a flood in Ohio, an avalanche in the Cascades or the tragedy in Oklahoma City, Harry and his search-and-rescue dog teams were there to help. In eight years of work, MWSD teams have performed 650 search-and-rescue missions and have saved more than 100 lives. Harry, who trained 1,000 dog-and-handler teams during his career, noticed something special in the eyes of the Newfy mix that cold winter day.

Harry needed to find a fitting name for his new dog. His son, Brandon suggested Ranger, after a popular Disney cartoon character that saves people in distress. "That's it! We'll call him Ranger."

Harry recruits all his dogs from animal shelters, "Shelter dogs make the best search-and-rescue dogs because they are so willing to please. I think they realize they have been saved. They try harder and they bond faster," says Harry. "When I visit a shelter, I evaluate a dog's temperament and health. I look for a dog that is inquisitive and playfully assertive. Ranger passed the test with flying colors. I like the fact he was of mixed breeding. He has the strength of the Newfoundland and the heart of the Labrador."

Search-and-rescue dogs must be highly trained and skilled. Ranger embarked on a program beginning with basic obedience training. At first, Ranger did what all dogs do until instructed otherwise: He went to the bathroom inside the house, chewed on chairs and performed other acts of uncivilized conduct. It didn't take Ranger long, however, to grasp Harry's rules and accept his leadership. The problems disappeared.

Harry never utilizes harsh training techniques on his dogs. If Ranger did not obey on first command, he was gently placed in position. As soon as Ranger obeyed, an immediate love reward of praise, stroking, hugs or kisses was granted. Ranger learned to respond in a positive manner around people and other animals. They worked together, they played together, and when the day was done, they slept together on the same bed.

Ranger liked the work. He soon advanced to off-leash commands, sign language, whistle commands and agility exercises. Ranger was eager and willing to perform. He learned to swim white-water rapids; track scents; sniff out victims buried under dirt, snow or debris; rappel from cliffs, climb ladders; and crawl through tight spaces and scattered rubble. He conquered mountains, deserts, jungles and water.

Smell is very important to a search dog. Ranger learned the art of tracking, trailing, air-searching and water recovery. He developed the ability to distinguish scents. A dog's sense of smell is 500 times better than man's, which is why they are used in search-and-rescue work. Smoking is not allowed around Mountain Wilderness Search dogs, since nicotine interferes with a dog's ability to smell. It takes a dog eight hours to recover its full sense of smell after being around a smoker.

A person or animal sheds approximately 1000 pieces of scent per day. To track someone, Ranger is introduced to a 'scent article,' like a shoe or sock at the 'point last seen.' He examines the area for smells. If he matches a smell with the scent article he "alerts." General searches require search dogs to alert at the sign of any victim. If a human is buried beneath debris, his scent ascends to the surface. If Ranger finds a person alive he becomes animated. He wags his tail, barks and begins to dig. If he smells death, he appears upset. His tail goes between his legs and he paws at the surface with little enthusiasm.

A successful dog handler must communicate well with his dog and pay close attention to the dog's signals. In rain, scents are washed into the ground and diluted, requiring the dog revert to air-scenting techniques. Harry pays constant attention to wind, wind shifts and land contour while reading Ranger's body language for positive scent identification. The dog and handler track the scent, carried by the wind, to reach their quarry. If the wind shifts and they don't respond, they could lose their pursuit.

Another form of search, water recovery, requires Ranger to survey the water in the area downstream from the 'point last seen.' He alerts when he smells the victim's decaying body odor lingering on the water's surface.

"For best results, searches should start within 24 hours," said Harry. Mountain Wilderness Search Dog teams are on-call to go anywhere, any time, in any type of weather. MWSD specializes in night searches. Volunteers are summoned from their warm beds to come to the aid of people in crisis at all hours of the night. Harry said, "Heat can dry out the scent. At night, people are stationary and the scent stays close to the ground. Most of our finds are during the night."

Harry assumes the air of a proud father when he describes Ranger's heroics.

His first assignment was to locate a drowning victim. "He located her within four minutes," Harry snapped.

Harry leaned back in his chair and began to reminisce. "One time while playing on a beach on the Oregon coast, I observed two little girls being swept out to sea by an undertow. Ranger and I went into the water. I caught one and the other held on to Ranger's harness as we swam them to safety." (Harry and Ranger received the MWSD Medal of Valor and North America Search And Rescue Water Rescue Award).

Harry & Ranger rappelling into a 90' crevasse.

"Another time, while working ski patrol on Oregon's Mount Hood, Ranger alerted. He took me to a remote area of the mountain where we found a hypothermic cross-country skier in shock. He was lying in the snow immobilized with a leg injury. Ranger, without command, proceeded to lie on the skier to provide warmth until the emergency medical team arrived."

"One of our more remarkable rescues involved looking for two missing mountain climbers. We went up in a helicopter in the area they were last seen. While flying, Ranger became agitated and began sniffing aggressively at the window. We noticed faint signs of tracks in the snow. We landed the helicopter to investigate. Ranger picked up a scent coming from a 90-foot-deep crevice. Ranger and I rappelled into the crevice. There, we found the missing climbers, injured from the fall. The climbers survived and have continually expressed their gratitude. All the hard work and training sure paid off that day."

"Ranger's sensitivity for people was uncanny. When working the Philippines earthquake in 1990, we found 59 victims. An aftershock hit. It caused a major mud slide that wiped out a village. A little girl, one of two survivors, lost her entire family. Ranger sensed the child's pain and loss and remained near her throughout the night, as she held and stroked him." Harry paused for a moment to collect himself. "He was a big comfort to her."

"One moment I'll never forget involved a therapy visit to a local children's hospital. There was a party going on and all the children were having fun. Ranger approached a sad and lonely little girl off by herself. She had burns over 95 percent of her body and facial disfiguration. Ranger wagged his tail, leaned up to her and gave her a wet, sloppy kiss. She wrapped her burned little arms around Ranger, hugged him and began to cry. Ranger laid in her arms until she quit crying. He stood up, wagged his tail, then gave her another wet kiss. She started laughing. The nurse told me, as we both wiped away tears, 'This was the first time the little girl has opened up and expressed emotion since her injury.' I told her, Ranger likes people no matter what they look like."

Harry and Ranger have ventured out into the cold, rainy nights to find endangered hunters lost in the woods, walked the urban streets to track wayward Alzheimer's patients and braved snowy mountains to locate lost children.

"Unfortunately there are times when we locate the remains of victims," said Harry. "One time we discovered the remains of a little boy who was a murder victim. I really took it hard. Ranger was there to comfort me. He helped me through it. There is a lot of tragedy in this line of work. We see the sick, injured, lost, scared and the dead. We deal with their friends and family. We experience the pain and suffering, too. Together, Ranger and I have shared it all."

Harry and Ranger initiated two community humanitarian programs. The Help US Find You program teaches children how to stay safe and, should they become lost, helps them survive the experience. Harry and Ranger have brought smiles to children's faces performing more than 1000 instructional programs for schools, camps and churches.

The Lost Pet Program utilizes the dogs' scent-training skills to search for lost and missing pets. Harry and Ranger tracked a missing dog five miles from home. They found him playing in a park. "Dog owners are elated when they are reunited with their lost pet," said Harry.

Ranger found 33 pets during his career. Harry started the Lost Pet Program not only as a community service but to keep the dogs sharp. "Ranger really enjoyed it" said Harry, "When Ranger worked in disaster situations he would become depressed when he found dead bodies. When we'd find a lost dog, he would become lively and animated. It's a positive exercise that reinforces his training."

In November 1994 pain from hip dysplasia became severe for Ranger. On the 25th of the month, Harry held Ranger in his arms. Ranger looked up and gave Harry one of his big sloppy kisses. Harry said good-bye as Ranger took his last breath and was put to rest.

Ranger touched many lives. A standing-room crowd of over 300 attended a commemorative service in the dog's honor. Hundreds more sent cards and letters. The music selected for the service included; *Born Free*, *Going Home*, *Over The Rainbow* and *Taps*. At the service Harry memorialized his best friend and partner:

"I held you in my arms today and I said good-bye. As I wiped the tears from my eyes I thought of all we have shared together. I think back to when we first met. When we saved you from the dog pound, your eyes full of love and happiness warmed our hearts and souls. You were there for me and Brandon and anyone else who needed you. You truly were sent here to us as a gift from God. The world and my heart have lost one gentle giant, my hero, you. I will forever hold you in my thoughts. The emptiness that you left will diminish but the love you shared will always stay."

– Harry Oakes, Your K-9 Partner, "K-9-1"

Ranger is one of the top Search And Rescue dogs of all time. He performed 370 missions with 157 finds, the International Search And Rescue record. He logged more than 20,000 hours of training. He lived up to his name by traveling over 250,000 miles in 25 states and six countries to perform his missions.

Ranger was decorated with the National Jefferson Award and the For Kids Sake Award. He was inducted into the Oregon Pet Hall of Fame. He was praised by Presidents George Bush and Bill Clinton for his worldwide accomplishments. Harry's and Ranger's heroism was featured on the TV show "Rescue 911."

Ranger was a fantastic Search and Rescue dog. He is also a shining example of the potential that exists in all shelter dogs. Harry Oakes had the knowledge and willingness to help Ranger realize his potential.

I wonder how many other Rangers are there in shelters waiting to be rescued?

Mountain Wilderness Search Dogs nonprofit volunteer group depends on private donation. To inquire about making a donation, contact: POB 30364, Portland, OR 97230-0364, (503) 650-1904

OUR TEACHER, OUR DOG

by Joseph Cerquone (Copyright © 1995 Joseph Cerquone)

As we waited for our veterinarian's injection to take hold on our dog, Opie, we tried to say our piece–our final goodbye. "Love you boy," we chorused as a family. "Thanks so much. We won't forget you."

Probably such things are said by many who stay with their pets to the end. But in Opie's case, the words had special meaning. For as I watched Opie's brown eyes slowly close, I also saw my foster children, two kids who know much human rejection, bidding farewell to the most dependable creature in their lives.

"He always kissed me three times!" one of them likes to say emphatically.

Experts concur on what the children know. "Many times, kids at risk have experienced a lot of sadness. They haven't been around people they trust," explains Earl Strimple, a veterinarian and president of People, Animals, Love, a Washington-based group that works with District youth. "But animals are responsive," Strimple points out. "They're something to have faith in."

Opie, though, was unique. He had natural "animal magnetism," but he also knew what it was like to be an outcast. When we adopted him, he had spent five years in a shelter for homeless dogs and cats; his history of living among the unwanted bonded him with kids like nothing else could have.

Naturally, we would have preferred that Opie never suffered that treatment, but we tried to use it as a positive lesson. For example, during family talks, with Opie lying by serenely, adult counsel often went like this: "Keep your chin up. You see what a great dog Opie is–he's a fine animal no matter what the world thought of him. So don't let anyone tell you you're not good enough."

Or: "Try not to be bitter. Look at Opie, He was rejected constantly, yet he found a way to remain gentle."

Indeed, thinking about life in the mix of Opie and our foster kids, I find it hard to easily summarize the important connection that were made–there were so many. In fact, one child might not have moved in at all had Opie not been with us. The dog put him at ease and got him to trust humans again, a prospect that can be scary and seem impossible to a foster child.

Bonding was everywhere with Opie in the house. It was symbolized by the dog statuettes in the children's rooms, and the pictures of the pooch that littered the pages of the kids' photo albums. Also there were family times watching movies like "Homeward Bound," where a character reminds us of Opie, or laughing over the get-ups loving owners put on their hounds for Alexandria's annual St. Patrick's Day parade. Opie even helped the kids with their schooling. He served as a subject for more than one writing assignment, homework that otherwise might have been neglected. Meanwhile, lessons about responsibility came in the form of animal care, chores willingly done because Opie was such a popular family member.

Even having a great dog can't erase all the rough spots. At my house, disagreements are unique, because there is no built-in biological basis for getting along; everyone must work a bit harder at forgiveness. Sometimes when there was a problem, the kids got through being upset because of Opie. "If he likes it here, I guess it can't be so bad after all" seemed to be their feeling.

Everyone wanted to be present when Opie was put to sleep. He was still well enough to display his charm: Though lame and cancer-stricken, on his last day he pushed himself to roll over and face us as we all sat at the kitchen table, sad-eyed. It was as though he heard duty calling him to be central to another family discussion. At a deeper level, choosing to euthanize Opie was tough because we knew it would mean losing the warm neutral core to our makeshift family.

"No!" is what I heard when the kids were told Opie's time had come. But they understood eventually, after they felt the lumps in his throat and heard his constant panting.

Often putting an animal to sleep is "much harder on the owner," according to Millie Bobbitt of the Alexandria Animal Welfare League. But Bobbitt stresses that "the important thing is to do what is best for the pet."

In the months since Opie's death, we've wept and ached. But we now have a new family member, a Washington Humane Society hound.

Part of us worried whether we were being disloyal getting another dog so quickly. But in the end, we chose to act on Opie's legacy: After all we had opened our hearts to the worth of unwanted animals.

Opie, you would have been happy to hear what one of the children said when we brought the new dog home: "Look, Dad," he exclaimed, excited by the steady wag in the animal's tail, "he likes me!"

SHANDY: FROM SHELTER TO SHOW-BIZ!

By Karen Meldrum

Animal Friends Magazine, Oakland SPCA

It began in 1982 when Shandy, a Golden Retriever mix who had been badly treated by his former owners, was surrendered to our shelter because he was "just too much trouble." Sapir Weiss, then a dog trainer in Oakland, came to the shelter with his wife, Jane, looking for a dog he could train as a family pet. He had in mind a regal dog, like their pedigreed German Shepherd, Tamarac. But they went home instead with Shandy, a playful, rough-and-tumble little guy who was irresistible to Jane when he sat up and begged to be chosen.

At first Shandy conducted his own one-dog demolition derby in the Weiss household. But Sapir's consistently firm and patient training methods eventually paid off, and Shandy became a welcome addition to the family.

Soon after, Sapir and Jane went to live in Israel, where he opened a training school. When he received a call asking if he had a dog that could appear in TV commercials, he was sure Tamarac would be perfect. When the TV commercials aired, Shandy stole the show and eventually the hearts of the Israeli people.

Using the stage name of Shteker, he appeared in a series of government commercials on energy conservation. He was shown in various situations in the home, closing refrigerator doors, turning off lights and so on. After each explanation of some energy-saving action, his co-star would ask, "Do you understand, Shteker?" These words would soon become a national phrase, much like "Where's the beef?" in this country.

Shandy was seen every day on television and appeared in newspapers, magazines, and even on bumper stickers. He was earning $600 per day, putting him in a 65% tax bracket. At one point, he became ill and reports of his food intake, temperature, and condition appeared daily in all the newspapers. Shandy was truly a national celebrity.

Then in 1985, Sapir and Jane decided to return to the United States. The Israeli Department of Energy first tried to gain custody of Shandy to keep him in Israel. Later, they relented on the condition that he remain a few months longer than the rest of the family to fulfill the remainder of his contract. When Shandy finally left the country, there was a huge farewell party at a fancy hotel attended by the rich and famous, including three ministers of the Israeli government.

It was a party to remember for Shandy, the dog to remember — the dog that went from an unwanted and discarded dog at the Oakland SPCA to a famous and pampered national celebrity!

But Shandy was glad to get home, back to his family. After all, that's where every dog belongs — with a family that loves him. And that's just where he is now, living out his retirement years with Sapir, Jane and their two children.

So the next time you're looking for a dog for your family, go to your local shelter, where you'll find dogs of every size, shape, and description. You're sure to find a companion and a friend for life. And who knows, you might even find a Shandy!

SHERLOCK

By Sonja

Finally I had reached my thirteenth birthday and my father said I could get a pet. I wasn't looking for a little puppy to play with; I was yearning for a friend to have with me for years. I was living in a home with a fenced-in back yard. I was willing to give up my free time to work and care for the animal's needs. I knew that I would have to do more than put out food; I would have to put out love.

My parents accompanied me to the local humane society to help find a dog that would be a good friend to me, and me to him/her. I had an idea that a small dog would be best. We looked at all the cute little puppies, and then we spotted one off by himself who was older than the others. No one seemed to be looking at him, but I couldn't resist his beautiful brown eyes. He was already four months old and weighed 20 pounds — a lot bigger than I had imagined for my dog.

He sat quietly, not calling to me like the other puppies and dogs. He even seemed disinterested in me. After all, his heart had already been broken once when he was left at the shelter. But I couldn't help myself and fell in love. I made arrangements for him to come home with us as soon as he was neutered. I paid the $50 adoption fee.

Sherlock has been with me for four years now and has turned out to be my best friend (even though he chewed everything in sight the first few months). My dad says it's lucky we adopted him, confiding that years earlier he worked in conjunction with a university on research into human-heart failure. The researchers used dogs from shelters for experiments, especially ones with large chests.

Sherlock has a large chest — to hold his large heart!

LOST AND FOUND

By Elizabeth Nicoloff

A year ago, I bought Sappho, a beautiful Belgian Tervuren. She lived in a small town in Northern California called Woodland, 500 miles from my home. Rather than have her shipped to La Jolla, where I live, I drove north to fetch her.

On the homeward trip, as I passed by San Luis Obispo on Highway 101 in midafternoon, I dozed. Whoof! I was off the road, back on the road, then off again, and the car came to rest in a grassy area between the north and south lanes of the highway.

The officials told me it had rolled over, but I was unaware of that. My beautiful car was totaled, but, more importantly, my dog was gone. California Highway Patrol and ambulance people swarmed over me almost instantly. They told me not to move. They were taking me to the hospital.

"I'm not leaving until you find my dog," I said.

"Lady, we are not going to stay here all afternoon," replied the chief ambulance person, at which point they strapped me to a litter, shoved it into the ambulance, and bore me off to the hospital. They kept me there two days "for observation," although my only injury was a seat belt bruise.

It came time to leave, but there still was no word of Sappho. In desperation, thinking perhaps she had been found injured and taken to a veterinarian for treatment instead of being turned in to the animal shelter, I began calling veterinarians in the area. On my third call, the girl who answered and heard my story asked, "You own a Tervuren?"

"I did," I responded, "for about two days, but I don't know where she is now."

"I own Tervurens," she said.

I asked her if she knew someone in Tervuren rescue. "I am!" she exclaimed. So I left the situation in her hands and rode sorrowfully home, sure that I wouldn't see my dog again and hoping she would fall into the hands of someone who would care for her and give her a good home.

As I walked in the door at home, the phone was ringing. It was the girl from San Luis Obispo.

"We found your dog!"

This wonderful person had organized a search party, and the searchers had found Sappho not far from the site of the accident, covered with ticks after two days in the wild and waiting for someone to come get her. A week later my dog and I were reunited, and she has become my truly devoted companion. The wonderful woman is named Sandy Weston. I have never met her, but I regard her as one of my dearest friends.

Editor's note: Elizabeth is 70 years young. She is active in competitive obedience. She and Sappho have earned their first and second stage obedience titles (CD and CDX) and are currently working on their UD title. They make a wonderful team.

IN PRAISE OF OLDER PETS

By Sherrie C. Woodbury

He lay huddled and shivering in his cage. Animal Control officers had picked him up as he wandered the streets, perhaps trying to get back to the home that had been his for the first eight years of his life.

With a filthy coat and a runny nose, he lacked "curb appeal." He was passed over by all the people looking for a perky puppy. On the day he was to be euthanized because nobody had adopted him, he was picked up by Little Angels Pug Rescue.

After a trip to the vet and groomer, Buddy Boy, the name given to him by his new owners, was ready to become a loving and devoted member of a family who would value his loyalty and affection. He now shares a recliner with his new "Daddy," Jess Sias, each evening and snuggles contentedly under the covers with him when it's time to go to bed.

Buddy Boy is one of the 30 percent of Pugs who are eight years and older when rescued. Pets like him are often not the first choice of prospective pet owners, but no one who has opened their homes and their hearts to one of these senior citizens has regretted the decision for a moment.

Johna Madigan, who adopted a 14-year-old Pug named Sarah Lee, speaks most eloquently about the joys of making a home for an older animal: "Age has nothing to do with what makes a pet worthwhile. A lot of people hesitate to choose an older dog, because they're afraid it won't be with them as long as they'd like. But by passing up a mature dog, they deny themselves the very special pleasures these dogs hold. Sarah is not a foolish little puppy. She has a unique presence that enriches our lives daily."

Perhaps no sight is sadder than an older dog or cat waiting at an animal shelter for someone to recognize the unique spirit that comes from a great deal of living. These animals are often housebroken and trained. They are calmer than younger animals and have a lifetime of loyalty left to give.

Why do these older animals need new homes? Sometimes an owner has died. Perhaps the owner is moving into a convalescent facility or a retirement residence where pets are not allowed. Often the specific reason is unknown, only that a faithful and loving pet is in jeopardy at a time in its life when it needs — and has earned — extra love and kindness for years of devotion.

When you're ready to add a new pet to your home, consider taking an animal in its golden years. Just ask Laura Boughn and Eric Gallegos about their eight-year-old adopted Buddie.

"We never dreamed what an impact our little dog would make in our lives," they comment. "We love him more than we ever imagined. He goes everywhere with us and is the most wonderful little friend."

When you're touring the shelter, take a second look at that dog or cat who's been around the block a few times.

Johna Madigan sums up the benefits of adopting an older pet. "No matter how long or short her stay is," she smiles as she strokes her 14-year-old dog's head, "it is a pleasure to have her in our home."

HE WAITED FOR YOU

Pet Press Newsletter
Southwest Missouri Humane Society

He was there when the staff came to work that morning, a black-and-white Border Collie mix, lying near the entrance gate. As each staff car pulled in, he got up and intently peered into the car, then turned away at the sight of an unfamiliar face to lie down again. *He was looking for you.*

All that day staff members and volunteers tried to coax him away from the entrance road. They were afraid a car pulling into the entrance would hit him or that he would wander the short distance to I-44 and get hit there. Each time he was approached, he would run into the woods, to reappear only after the person left to resume his vigil at the entrance gate. *He was waiting for you.*

That evening when the shelter closed he was still there, so food and water was left at the entrance for him. The next morning, he was still there. He still examined each car coming into the entrance but would occasionally roam toward the shelter, so the staffers renewed their efforts to gain his confidence. He still would not be approached, and as closing time neared, the staff again left him food and water. *He was still waiting for you.*

The third day came and he was still there. On the advice of a veterinarian, he was given a mild tranquilizer in some food. The staff kept a watch on him, and finally in midafternoon he wandered into an area where gates could be closed behind him. He tried to flee, but the tranquilizers had slowed him down.

You wanted him once. He was probably a very cute puppy. Did he grow up to be a barker and disturb the neighbors? He never barked while *Waiting for you* here. Did you find he was too expensive to feed and care for? You didn't have to dump him. We depend on donations to take care of our animals, but if you couldn't afford to leave a donation, we would still have taken him. But our hearts went out to him as we watched him *waiting for you.*

Technically, he is a stray, and by law we must hold him for five days. At the end of that time he will be evaluated, and if his experience of being "dumped" hasn't traumatized him too much, he will be put up for adoption.

We hope to find him a good home, perhaps someone who would cherish the thought of a loyal, loving dog there *waiting for them to come home*.

MINKA & SANDY

By Ms. Clyde Freeman
The American Humane Association, Englewood, CO

"Hey Mom, let's consider getting a dog," my daughter said recently.

"You must be joking. I am too busy to take care of a dog, and my life is stressful enough."

"A dog actually might relieve some of the stress," she countered.

On my next day off, I went to the municipal pound just to take a look, not expecting to see a dog I'd want to take home that day. In one of the cages was the scroungiest, dirtiest dog with the saddest but most loving eyes I've ever seen. A true Heinz 57 mix, he looked to be part poodle, part Fox Terrier, and I rushed home to get my daughter so she could see him.

"Mom, this dog is the most pitiful, horrible dog in the whole shelter. Why do you like him?"

I could not explain why I liked this particular dog but asked her to imagine him all cleaned. Instead, she scouted the shelter for another dog.

"Hey, Mom," she rushed back. "I found the dog. We'll call her Minka. She's a Chihuahua mix, and you've got to see her."

Minka was licking her hand through the bars and giving her a variety of mournful, pleading whines. We took both dogs to the bonding room, and I told my daughter we'd have to choose one.

"That's easy. We'll take Minka," said my daughter.

The shelter attendant came in to take my scraggly, sad-eyed friend, but tears built up inside me, so I called him back and let him know that we were still deciding. This scene occurred two more times, before we came to the conclusion that we wouldn't be happy without both dogs. To think that I'd had serious questions about adopting one dog, and now we would have two.

Now we can't imagine life without them. No matter what has occurred during the day, it is always special to be greeted at the door by Sandy and Minka. Adopting two dogs can be even more fun than adopting one, and they keep each other, as well as us, company.

ADOPTING A SPECIAL-NEEDS DOG

By Cheryl Minnier

As adoption coordinator, I get two kinds of applications from people who want to adopt our Goldens: people who have an idea of the perfect Golden in their minds and want help finding him, and people who just want to help "whoever needs me most," warts and all. It is for these people that I thought I would write the story of Moses.

I got a call one day from a friend who works in a shelter about a Golden "who didn't look good." Some kids had found him lying in a field and noticed he hadn't moved for two hours. Luckily, my friend recognized a Golden under the dirt and sores and in spite of the fact that he had almost no hair. He weighed 63 pounds on a frame that now comfortably holds 104.

I make it a rule not to become overly attached to my temporary "guests." I have seven dogs of my own and have never considered keeping a rescue dog. Something happened though when I took this dog out of the kennel at that shelter. He walked over to me and leaned against my side, giving me a look that said, "In spite of what's happened to me, and even though I have every reason not to, I'm putting my trust in you."

Every time an adoptive home would be mentioned for Moses, I had a good reason it wouldn't work. At first he was just too sick with every known parasite. He hadn't eaten for so long he could only hold down one teaspoon of food an hour. His skin was a massive staph infection, his back was covered with weeping sores, and his ear was swelled shut by an untreated hematoma.

As these things cleared up, I was running out of excuses not to place him when he had his first seizure. I am a nurse with a lot of experience, but I panicked, thinking he was dying and rushed to the phone to call a vet I knew. When I left the room, Moses tried to follow me by dragging himself across the floor on his belly. By the time the vet calmed me down and said it sounded like a localized seizure, Moses was fine, wagging his tail and asking for a cookie. I, however, took the rest of the day to recover.

This episode was the final straw. "Nobody will want him now," I said. "So he's got to stay." Moses became ILP Stonehills Out of the Wilderness and an official part of the Minnier household. He's had a few more seizures and also episodes of vomiting with no warning, but they never seem to bother him for long. We've all learned to ride them out with him, and even my children are no longer bothered by them. My vet and those at Cornell seem to feel the seizures are from an area of localized brain damage, perhaps from being kicked or struck in the skull at one time and are not likely to ever get worse.

I realize Moses doesn't sound like the dog of most people's dreams. I have seven other dogs, all of whom love me best in the world. But none of them looks at me the way Moses does. When I am home, he is never out of reach, not underfoot but always somewhere close enough to touch me or settle at my feet if I sit down. It's as if he can't believe he found me and wants to make sure he isn't going to lose me. He is the most enthusiastic, obedient dog I have ever seen and will respond instantly to a slight nod of my head or a shift of my hand position, even to commands whispered from across a room — anything to make me happy.

In return for this worship, we just make sure he always has someone to stay with him when he has a seizure. We keep the bugs away from him, because he seems deadly afraid of them, probably from being chained out for so long. We always let him know what we expect from him and never let pity get in the way of teaching him how to behave. He has learned to trust that we will keep him safe, and he knows he can look to us when he is unsure of anything. The world once again (or maybe for the first time) makes sense to Moses.

TOPPER

Delta Society Service Dogs of the Year
Interactions Magazine 1994

"Topper is soft, cuddly and quiet. There's not a bite in him!"

That's the way Topper's owner, Ann Whitton, describes the spunky sable-and-white Sheltie. But Topper is much more than that. A veteran of serious illness himself — he had bone disease and hip surgery when just a pup — he pioneered the Delta Pet Partners Program skills and aptitude requirements for visiting hospitals and nursing institutions.

Ann and Topper regularly visited a California psychiatric hospital, where Topper attended group therapy sessions. From the outset, Topper exhibited a unique ability to relate to patients, his non-threatening nature and calm presence allowing the patients to leave their own inner turmoil and focus on, and smile at, this gentle dog.

His greatest triumph was with a young woman who could not communicate at all. At her first group session, Topper went right to her, seeming to sense her need. The patient took him in her arms and cried and cried — a real breakthrough in her treatment. From that day on, he always went directly to the woman; on each visit, she held him tightly, saying, "Topper takes my pain away."

But as she improved, he went to her less and less, seeming to understand that she no longer needed him. Upon her release, the patient vowed it was this loving dog that had contributed to her "true miracle" recovery.

MUGGS

By Rosemary Shelton

I found her in the morning when I arrived for work at the Escondido Humane Society. She had been left outside the gate, no name, no owner identification, no age, nothing. A very pregnant German Shepherd mix, she had everything going against her.

Two days after arriving, she gave birth to nine puppies. She wasn't much of a mother because she leaped up from feeding the pups every time someone came by, seeming to consider it her duty to greet every human she ever encountered. Whenever someone stopped to talk to her, she would smile, curl back her lips and show

Photo by Click, the Photo Connection

her teeth. I started calling her Muggs. She quickly became a favorite with the kennel staff, not just because she was so friendly, but also because she was gentle and obedient.

These traits led me to beg for her to be placed in the adoption program, despite the fact that she was quite thin, a dirty gray in color and rather ugly looking. My pleas were heard, and she was moved into an adoption cage.

The very things that endeared Muggs to the staff and volunteers were overlooked by the public because of her appearance. Also, when she smiled at them, they thought she was snarling and quickly moved to the next kennel. She languished in the adoption kennels for three months.

I took a special interest in her and went to great lengths to find her a home. I was in charge of the Sunday adoption event at a local mall. For three Sundays in a row I took the ugly Shepherd mix in hopes she would find a home. Muggs didn't travel in the back of the van with the others; she sat up front between the driver and passenger. She never created a problem. She also didn't get adopted.

One day a shelter staff member approached and told her that Muggs' time was up, that other dogs needed a chance. I knew I couldn't let that happen. I decided to take Muggs home and foster her until I could place her. The first stop was the groomer's. When I returned for Muggs, I found a beautiful tricolored Shepherd with lovely markings.

It took just two days for Muggs to work her magic. My husband and I decided we could never give her up. She gained weight. Exercise slowly built up her muscles. The ugly duckling nobody wanted became a swan, as well as the most gentle, loving, obedient and sweet-natured animal that I had ever met. She became our adored companion. Where we went, she went, including vacations. She gave us many fun-filled years of pleasure.

This throwaway dog that no one else wanted is gone now. I'm still inclined to look for her beside the bed, or expect her wagging tail when I arrive home. Her ashes are carefully buried under her favorite spot in the yard, leaving behind an aching void in the lives of the only people who did want her.

JOE, ASSISTANCE DOG

Delta Society Dog of the Year 1993
Interactions Magazine

Joe was an unruly, mixed-breed stray destined for euthanasia at the Humane Society of Seattle and King County when he was given a second chance. A registered nurse whose mobility had been impaired by multiple sclerosis since 1978, Susan Duncan needed an assistance dog for security and independence.

Susan brought Joe home and trained him intensively for six months, transforming the former renegade into a "calm, reliable assistant."

"He has taken over the tasks I couldn't do easily by myself — pulls the covers off in the morning and helps me get out of bed," says Susan.

Joe helps her up and down steps and ramps and, if she falls, helps her to stand. He locates her car when she forgets where it's parked and pulls the wheelchair if the battery dies. Joe also finds the curb cuts and keeps Susan from walking in front of cars when her vision is impaired.

And when Susan's illness brings on understandable frustration, Joe plays the clown. He opens the dishwasher, pulls out the racks, upends his metal food bowl and bats it across the floor.

"It's impossible to remain introspective through all that," says Susan.

CHAMP

By Stephanie Cooley
Pomona Valley Humane Society

Dan Prestby of Fontana, who had already adopted two cats from the shelter, came in looking for a third. For some inexplicable reason he was drawn to the dog kennels, where he encountered Judy, a black Australian Shepherd/Sheltie mix. A wag of her little tail convinced him to take her home as soon as she became available for adoption.

Like many shelter animals, Judy had some problems adjusting at first. She was fearful of walking up steps or even going from a tiled area to a carpeted area at home. Mr. Prestby had heard that agility training could help dogs overcome confidence problems, and he enrolled Judy in a course.

Judy blossomed in agility, and her true nature emerged. She recently defeated 94 other dogs to become Western Region Agility Champion and will compete for the national title later this year. She also discovered competitive sheepherding and has two "legs" toward a sheepherding title. "All this," says Dan Prestby, "from a little, black, 27-pound dog that no one wanted!"

GRADY O'GRADY

By Eugene E.W. Pei, D.V.M.
Denver Municipal Animal Shelter

The early morning air outside the shelter is still cool and fresh. A sparrow chirps a cheerful "good morning," interrupted only by faint barks echoing inside the shelter walls. Armed with *the Rocky Mountain News* and a cup of coffee, I settle down for a two-hour wait. As I attempt to concentrate on the day's news, my attention strays to the barking, and I check my watch. The owner of one of those faint barks awaits adoption at the magical hour of 8 a.m. The empty parking lot confirms my hope that I'll be first in line.

At last the time has come, and the doors open. After a painless bit of paperwork, I open a cage door and gingerly lift 5.5 pounds of Yorkie into my arms. It's as if he instinctively knows he is in a pair of "safe" arms and is on his way home.

Grady, the inquisitive Yorkie with the bright eyes and the button nose, may be but a smidgen of a dog, but he gallantly rises to the occasion. With a determined strut, he enters his new home, investigates its far corners and conveys his approval with a slight tilt of his head. After a momentary break to sample a few morsels of kibble and several laps of fresh water, Grady continues on to investigate. He finds in the corner the fluffiest pillow ever, a comfy place for a quiet snooze.

As the warmth of the summer day surrenders to a cool evening breeze, I sit near an open window. Almost imperceptibly Grady jumps onto the couch, circles intently once or twice to find just the right spot, then curls up as close as possible to my left thigh. I glance down to see his head tilted slightly, eyes gazing intently upward toward mine. He shifts his weight to allow himself to move even closer to my leg, rests his head on his paws, closes his eyes and sighs contentedly as if to say, "I'm home." I agree wholeheartedly.

"HIP, HIP, HOORAY, MY HIP'S GONNA BE OK!"

By Diane Dynis
Mile High Humane Society

Bad news: The X-rays showed a crushed pelvis. The shelter vet said the little lost Chihuahua needed surgery ASAP, but money was tight for the nonprofit Mile High Humane Society.

On May 25, 1995, a man had somehow noticed the soaking wet little lump lying on the side of the road and had taken him to the society, where they named him Yoda. Shelter staffers hoped a media appeal would help, and the outpouring of love and concern for a little dog with big ears and a limp overwhelmed them. Hundreds of calls came in from all over Colorado, even from Wyoming and California, offering donations and a new home. Even better, an orthopedic surgeon, Dr. Guy Newton of Peak Animal Hospital, offered to perform the surgery at his cost right away!

Not long after successful surgery, Yoda went home with Mr. and Mrs. Dan Lowman of Aurora, feeling special since so many people wanted to adopt him and they didn't even know him. Guess that's where the term "lucky dog" comes from!

Thanks to the generosity of many caring humanitarians, a fund was established with the extra donations to care for the medical needs of other indigent animals.

ACTIVITY DOG, GRACIE

Interactions Magazine

A brindle-and-white whippet, Gracie was a "skinny dog knocking at doors" when she was picked up by Animal Control. Her future came in the form of Kit Jenkins of the Atlanta Humane Society, who saw Gracie's potential. After careful testing and training, Gracie was ready for her new job as the society's "education dog" and mascot.

Gracie quickly learned the names of staff members and friends, developing a vocabulary of some 425 words and phrases. Her job duties include regular visits to area schools, nursing homes and health care institutions, brightening countless lives. As a testimony to her abilities, Gracie's nomination for the Delta Dog of the Year award included a joint endorsement from all the residents of Ansley Pavilion Nursing Home — "We vote for Gracie!"

Gracie comes to the facility and knows she has a job to do. She brings joy and love to everyone, and as she makes her rounds, never missing a room, she brings laughter to some who have not laughed in weeks, according to Charlotte Beverly, activity director at Fairburn Health Care Center.

GINGER'S STORY

By Alice Adams

I never thought "shelter dogs" were a good idea, assuming that any dog from a shelter must be a throwaway, either unmanageable, untrained, mean or sick. Now, I know better. With an adult dog you skip many of the puppy problems. Shelter dogs are wonderful dogs to adopt. I know!

My shelter-adopted dog is Ace's Ginger Snap Cookie, a 10-pound Pekinese/Cocker love sponge. She has cream-colored hair on her head, shading to a rich ginger-brown on her tail, with big, Cocker booties on her feet. I adopted Ginger in May 1994. She was scheduled for destruction the very next day.

Ginger is probably the best dog I have ever had. She is quiet, housebroken, loyal, loving, calm, loves to go "walkies" (you can't even whisper the word in the house), polite to strangers, and, incidentally, blind. Yes, even though she is only about 3 1/2 years old, she has well-developed cataracts in both eyes and is now almost totally blind. No matter. She does "hot-laps" with the other two dogs, as she knows every inch of the house and the yard, and runs full tilt around every tree, bush and flowerpot in the garden. On our neighborhood walks, she trusts me to keep her out of trouble and never hesitates to walk when and where I tell her.

In January 1995, Ginger found her true calling. My daughter had a baby, and they both live with me. Ginger took it upon herself to make sure the baby is always all right. Whenever we are outside with the baby, no matter where anyone else is in the yard, Ginger is oh so casually seated right next to, but not close enough to get her ears pulled by the baby. Normally she comes inside when I do, except when the baby is outside. I intend to have her certified as a therapy dog. She has enough love for everyone.

A NEW LEASH ON LIFE

The Wayfarer, Summer 1995

Berkeley East Bay Humane Society

Bubba came into the shelter in February of 1994 at an adolescent 10 months. The excuse for surrendering him was that he "couldn't get along with other dogs," when he actually gets along fine with other dogs and loves people. But he was completely unsocialized and apparently unfamiliar with everything that goes on in the real world. He was afraid of absolutely everything. When out on walks, he would panic and spin, crashing into your legs, at the sight of anyone nearer than a block away.

He stayed at the back of his kennel during viewing hours and was repeatedly passed over for adoption. A big, shaggy black dog lying against a back kennel wall is not really going to get much consideration by people looking for a pet.

By October, we were beginning to despair about what to do with him. It didn't seem possible to find him a home, and we faced a time when it would no longer be humane to allow him to languish in the kennel. He needed a lot of special work, and a nice home alone would not solve his problems.

It was about that time that trainer Elen Weiss, who teaches our obedience classes, noticed him. She recognized what a truly nice and loyal companion he could be if his fearfulness could be overcome. She contacted Nancy Frensley, who was developing a formal volunteer program for the shelter. Together, they devised a training plan for Bubba to be carried out by volunteers and staff.

Within two months, the training began to make a difference. He became accustomed to different sights and sounds. Positive obedience training gave him a way to cope with all the fearful stimuli of the outside world. It took the vigilant efforts of staffers and volunteers working together for seven months to bring Bubba to a state where he could be adopted. He and his new partner attend Weiss' obedience classes together.

The work with Bubba became the basis for the Shelter Animal Volunteers for Enrichment (SAVE) program. Bubba has a home, and, because of Bubba, other dogs are receiving the special attention needed to become more adaptable and better able to fit into their new homes.

BEN & JERRY

By Beth Magnus

I came home from work that Tuesday still on a high from my weekend of skiing in Stowe, Vermont. The blinking red light from my answering machine beckoned me. Wing, my mixture of Golden Retriever and Sheltie of 16 years, followed me to hear the message.

"Beth, there's a Corgi at the shelter. I put it on reserve for you so no one else could take it. Call me so I know what to do. Bye!" said Bonnie.

My heart started to beat loudly. I've been looking for more than 10 years, off and on, at the shelters in the area for a Corgi. Each time I saw a Corgi in the pet shop or at the local dog shows, I would check out the shelter again but with no luck. Bonnie had taken care of Wing when I went skiing and was reminded that I've been looking for a Corgi. I knew Wing was getting old, and I always felt badly leaving her at home alone when I went to work.

I called Bonnie to find out if the Corgi was still there and drove the mile to the shelter, my head exploding with inner dialog. If it's a male and looks like Hank (my first Corgi when I was eight years old) I'll consider taking the dog. What will Wing think? Is this a good idea?

When I saw Bonnie, I asked if it was a male and she said yes as we walked toward the cage. Then I saw that foxy face — almost a Hank twin. Bonnie took the Corgi out and we went into a room. I made up my mind before I was kissed to death with the typical long Corgi tongue.

I found out his name was Benji and I said, "No problem I'll call him Ben." He was neutered, just 13 months old and was given up by an older couple. I assumed from Ben's exuberant behavior this was the cause for his departure from that environment.

I had never dealt with crating a dog before, but out of my fear of the older dog getting hurt or hurting Ben, I crated him when I was out. Wing, who also came from a shelter, had lost her hearing, which was good because Ben would try to herd her and barked all the time.

Four months later, I had to euthanize Wing. I would never have survived her loss without Ben.

In time Ben got a brother whom he first met at four weeks of age. His brother's name was Gus until a co-worker suggested the name Jerry.

Ben still has problems to work out, like his fear of thunder and strange noises, but I've seen improvement in him thanks to obedience classes. Ben's first "A" match was a hoot. On off-lead, we heeled on the command, then on right turn, Ben left the ring to pee for two minutes. I guess I didn't give him time to before we went into the ring. Ben returned with a beautiful sit. After the laughter died down, we got into position for the recall. I walked away praying for Ben to be in the sit position. I turned around, and he was. I yelled, "Ben come!" and he ran in full force toward me. I thought, "Oh, no!" as I knew he wasn't going to stop in time. Ben ran past me, kissed the spectators behind me and returned without a command for a straight sit. That's my Ben.

Seven months of training later Ben got his first leg. It was noisy, and the air conditioner sounded like thunder when it went on, but we did it. Ben achieved a Companion Dog title, Canine Good Citizen and is an active Therapy Dog International participant.

It's been three years since I picked up my rescue Corgi, Ben. Without him, I would not have Jerry or have become involved with the various dog clubs, with rescue or with working to educate people about the importance of spaying and neutering and on proper care of their pets.

A DOG NAMED HOPE

By Darris Hercs

Animal Friends Magazine, Oakland SPCA

Among the thousands of animals cared for and rehabilitated at the Oakland SPCA each year, certain cats and dogs touch us more deeply than the rest. Sometimes it is because the animals show great spirit despite the past difficulties they have experienced. They may be in pain, but they fight to get beyond it. They may be so abused that it takes a long, long time to reach them, but when some of the hardest to reach begin trusting, listening, answering to their names, we remember.

So it is with the three-year-old German Shepherd that staff members found standing at the entrance to the Oakland SPCA parking lot. Somebody had dropped the dog off and disappeared. Upon approaching the animal, our staffers immediately learned why. Her face was covered with boils, she had open sores on her ears from flea bites, she was some 40 pounds underweight, her paws were infected with foxtail tracks, and she had a serious hair-loss problem.

Was it guilt that finally drove the dog's owner to drop her off? Was it embarrassment that caused the owner not to own up to his/her irresponsibility and neglect? Was it fear of prosecution? Probably all of the above.

Besides her obvious problems, the veterinary staff discovered that the Shepherd (they named her Hope) was suffering from an infectious case of sarcoptic mange and a severe flea allergy dermatitis, that she was infested with roundworm and coccidiosis, and that a number of painful foxtails were embedded between her toes and in her ears.

Several months later, after a steady high-protein diet, a series of medicated flea baths, regular dips for the mange and lots of love from the shelter staff, Hope was adopted by a caring, wonderful new family — mine. As assistant director of the shetler, I see many animals I would like to take home.

DOING THE BEST WE CAN

By Laura Strickland
PET PALS of Florida Animal Rescue

She was thrown away in a garbage Dumpster.

She was four days old, her eyes still closed, her tiny paws smaller than my fingertips. Someone had wrapped the newborn puppy in a dark-colored bag and tossed her away like trash. No respect for life. No sympathy for the suffering she was about to endure as she starved to death or froze during the night in the frigid winter temperatures.

A couple who found her in the Dumpster tried to care for her, staying up all night to nurse the puppy every two hours. But they were working people and knew they couldn't keep up that schedule. They didn't want to take her to the pound, because they were afraid she would be put to sleep. So they brought her to us at PET PALS Animal Rescue, because they had heard we keep our animals until they find homes.

At four days of age, the puppy's chances of surviving were impossible. Abandoned newborn kittens and puppies almost never survive without a mother. They need a mother's milk and a mother's love.

Mika and Michelle, two teenage volunteers with Animal Rescue, named the puppy Lucky Shadoe (pronounced "shadow") and immediately fell in love with her. We all did. It worried me. If Lucky Shadoe didn't make it, our hearts would be broken.

A local television station, Channel 12, came out to film the abandoned "Dumpster" puppy, and calls poured in from people wanting to help the newborn. One man called to say he had a Dalmatian mother nursing two puppies of her own and volunteered to take Lucky Shadoe and see if the puppy would nurse from a surrogate mom.

The puppy's chances had just improved from impossible to possible.

A week later, Lucky Shadoe was doing well, having taken to the mother, and the mother, Queen of Hearts, having taken to the puppy. The surrogate mother nursed Lucky Shadoe, groomed her and guarded her from guests who tried to take a peek at the famous puppy.

Lucky Shadoe wasn't out of the woods, I knew. Less than two weeks old, she still had a struggle ahead. But with Queenie as her mom, the puppy's chances improved from possible to hopeful.

Every animal rescuer will tell you they give their hearts away every day to the animals they rescue. It's not easy being a rescuer. We go down to the pound when the animals are about to be put to sleep, and we rescue as many as we can. It is difficult to choose which ones to save and which ones to leave behind to face their fate — all because people do not spay or neuter their pets.

I cry in my car a lot as I drive away from the pound. Sometimes I can't sleep. Sometimes I feel like giving up. That's when I hear my grandmother's voice speak to me.

"Do the best you can and leave the rest up to God."

I live by those words every day.

FOUNDLINGS

By P. Parker

One evening I was passing my front door (door open/screen keeping out the flying beasties), when I noticed a patch of dirty white fur on my front step. Thinking it was the nasty neighborhood tom who had been ruining my evenings with his caterwauling and my screen with his spraying, I pushed open the screen prepared to shoo him away. To my surprise, two brown, limpid eyes looked up at me.

"And whose puppy are you?," I said, too late to save myself.

"I'm all yours, Mom," the pup said, albeit telepathically.

Someone had driven to my rather secluded hilltop, stopped their car, deposited the 3½-month-old puppy on the pavement, and drove off, leaving him to be adopted or to be coyote bait. It didn't matter to them which it would be.

At the time, my fence had a large breach and would not have kept an elephant in, much less a small and energetic puppy, so I prevailed on the people at the animal shelter to keep him safe until I could get the fence mended. One week (and one week's pay) later, I embarked on my career as a puppy mom.

The obedience club people insist that I refer to him as an all-American, but he really is your basic Terrier/cattle dog/some of this/some of that mutt. The love and pleasure I received from that little guy convinced me it was crazy to limit myself (and him) just to each other's company. After we'd been together for about four months, I found a female Lab mix through a local rescue group. He is all energy and action — she all snuggle and companionship. Imagine, if you will, a 53-pound "lap dog." They enjoy each other, and I enjoy them both more than I can say.

I have put a lot of money into feeding, medical care (neutering/spaying being a must), hardware (beds, toys, fencing), but not a dime was wasted. In fact, my castoffs are two of the best things ever to happen to me. For one who had previously never even wanted to have a companion dog, I now wonder how I ever survived without them and will never be without a dog again.

People need to see the joys of adopting "mutts," the very *best* dogs on Earth!

Photo by Linda Leeman

THE SHEPHERD'S SHEPHERD
By Ranny Green
Seattle Times Pet Columnist

"She's Saint Margaret," says Lyn Bingham, Seattle Purebred Dog Rescue director and a longtime friend of Margaret LaTour.

"Hundreds of German Shepherds owe their lives to her, and many families have a great pet as a result of her dedication. I don't know where we'd be without her."

If there is a German Shepherd heaven, rest assured Saint Margaret will be there to greet each of her flock coming home. LaTour is consumed with saving every area Shepherd possible, whether the case originates with a phone call at noon or midnight. Eight years of hard work were highlighted July 8 when a reunion of former adopters was organized.

"This is my payday," she exclaimed, as 32 dogs and their significant others showed up for a day of frolic, a fling at sheepherding under the guidance of Joe Kapelos. "This makes it all worthwhile," says LaTour, who occasionally might remember a dog's name before its owners'. "I was overwhelmed. If all owners were like the ones we had there, I'd be out of a rescue job."

For LaTour, it all began innocently enough when she was competing in an obedience trial in 1988. "Dale Gordon (an SPDR co-founder) asked if I had a couple hours a week to work on Shepherd rescue. I said 'yes.' Little did I know I'd be spending between 30 to 50 hours most weeks since then."

Since LaTour began rescue work, the number of dogs handled by SPDR has risen steadily: 1988, 59 dogs (September through December); 1989, 232; 1990, 269; 1991, 284; 1992, 323; 1993, 350; 1994, 318; and more than 170 in the first part of 1995.

There are some who claim this patron saint is married to the German Shepherd breed. But rest assured, she has a supportive husband, Tony, and daughters Sarah, 14, and Samantha, 13.

"There's a high divorce rate in rescue work," says LaTour, "but Tony and the girls have been very supportive. I won't deny we've had some pretty good battles over the amount of time I spend at it."

The phone rings day and night with people inquiring about Shepherd placement or relinquishment. Once she returned home to 17 voice-mail messages.

Even though Rottweiler overtook the Shepherd last year on the Seattle area's 10 Most Unwanted List, 332-318, LaTour believes her breed has been betrayed by the public, with such relinquishment excuses as divorce, moving, lack of time, dog's too big, dog sheds too much, dog's uncontrollable, etc.

"Don't get me wrong, there are legitimate reasons why people have to part with their dog, but most of the ones I hear are pretty lame. Have these people ever heard of commitment? When they bought that dog, they supposedly accepted a lifetime responsibility. That doesn't seem to mean much today."

Temperament, LaTour recognizes, is a suitable reasons for relinquishing a dog. "Have it checked by a professional," she suggests. "There are some ticking time bombs out there that are simply not fixable. "I saw about one dog per week with an irretrievable temperament," she adds. "That's the most ever.

What hurts more than anything is our failure to place dogs five and over. There are some polite middle-aged gentlemen and ladies that are euthanized simply because someone is tired of the responsibility. The other thing going against them is the appeal of puppies."

LaTour concedes the German Shepherd isn't for everyone: "It's a large breed that will control a household if you let it. The owner must assume the alpha role from the time he or she brings it home."

The July 8 fun day was a true reflection of LaTour's fan club. She drew smiles and hugs from just about everyone in her "extended family."

"Given a chance, these dogs have unlimited potential," says LaTour. "Seeing dogs like this come back is what helps keep me going."

LaTour has developed a close working relationship with Seattle area shelters. She has earned the respect of employees for her dedication and around-the-clock concern for Shepherd castoffs. She's called regularly when dogs are relinquished by owners. Many hard-to-place adoption candidates have been quartered longer than normal before scheduled euthanasia, in hopes LaTour can find suitable homes.

As one shelter worker put it, "If anyone can find a home for a German Shepherd in the Seattle area, Margaret can. She's a savior."

A WHOLE LOT OF SHAKING GOIN' ON

By Sherrie C. Woodbury
Little Angels Pug Rescue

Joanne Bush awoke to a low rumbling like the sound of a freight train bearing down on her house in Sylmar. Then the shaking began. A veteran of the 1971 Sylmar quake, she knew it was another quake — a major one. The shaking subsided, to be followed by four seconds of violent up-and-down movement that felt, she says, like an explosion. This one was much worse than 1971, she knew, so bad it must be the "Big One" that's been the stuff of nightmares for so many Californians for so many years.

She ran to the rear house where her mother lives to make sure the older woman was all right. Forcing open the door, she found a large double-door refrigerator upended and a dresser toppled onto her mother's bed. She didn't see her terrified Puggy, a four-year-old fawn Pug, slip out the door as she frantically dug her mother out from under the room's tumbled contents.

Half an hour later, after determining that the rest of her family and neighbors were alive, she noticed that the tiny Pug was missing. Frantic searching throughout the neighborhood failed to turn up Puggy. It was the beginning of four days of waiting and worrying and checking the animal shelters.

Finally, on the Thursday after the quake as she drove through her shattered town looking for her Pug, she saw a sign on a light post. A concerned motorist had found a shivering and frightened Pug about to cross a major intersection and had taken her home so that she wouldn't have to go to an overcrowded shelter.

Happily, it was Puggy, and she was reunited with her distraught family. In typical Pug fashion, the animal had taken over the home of her rescuers.

"They asked me if I knew she snored," Bush laughs. "The little dickens had been sleeping in bed with them and eating people food three meals a day."

Carolyn Colino and her husband also awoke to the violent shaking of the Northridge earthquake. Their home, located in Arleta several miles from the Bushes, was near the epicenter of the 6.8-magnitude quake that wreaked havoc throughout Southern California.

Rocky, their two-year-old black male Pug, panicked and ran out into the back yard as the quake struck. The Colinos were unaware that, like thousands of homeowners throughout the San Fernando Valley, they had lost their seemingly indestructible cement-block walls and wrought-iron fence to the quake.

Within minutes of the first powerful tremor, they ran outside to check on their Shar-pei and discovered that both dogs had escaped. They jumped into their car and began driving up and down streets within several miles of their home but found neither dog.

The Colinos checked shelters in the affected area daily and posted notices on street lights and telephone poles. A week passed by with no word of their pets. Just as they were about to give up hope, they received a call from Pat Robinson of Mission Hills. Rocky had run more than three miles, terrified by the movement of the earth, and the Robinsons had found him.

The Robinsons spotted one of the Colinos' fliers at a shelter and called to let them know their baby was safe. Still frightened, Rocky spends most of the time in his bed in the kitchen close to "Mom" and "Dad" Sadly, nearly two months after the quake, the Colinos still had not found their Shar-pei.

Of course the Robinsons fell in love with Rocky and now want to adopt a Pug of their own.

Unfortunately, other Pugs never found their people in the aftermath of the quake.

A small, black, female Pug had been found running beside the partially destroyed 118 Freeway. She ended up in a cage with four other dogs at a San Fernando Valley animal shelter. Two weeks after the shaker, her owners had still not come looking for her, and she was put up for adoption.

Her experiences had left her emaciated with kennel cough and whipworms. Little Angels Pug Rescue bailed her out, provided her with veterinary care and placed her (now called Molly) with the Cardillo family in Mission Hills. She has so entranced the household that they've adopted an eight-year-old female Pug named Elizabeth Taylor.

At the same shelter, an eight-year-old fawn male Pug waited dolefully for owners who never came. Also suffering from kennel cough and worms, he was rescued by Little Angels and placed almost immediately in a new home in Cerritos. He's lost no time in convincing his new owners, Mark Herriott and Charles Wise, as only Pugs can, that he needed to be fattened up immediately.

Despite the continued shaking, Chrisa Whiting and Loris Fusco, Little Angels volunteers, rescued and fostered the two Pugs who found their way to the shelter after the quake. They live in Reseda at the epicenter of the quake with their two-year-old black Pug, Rose, and Emma. Amid shattering glass from a sliding door that exploded in the initial shock, the Pug and people flew into the hallway. For the next several days they joined neighbors camping outside until it could be determined that their homes were safe.

"I had just taken Rose off her leash for the first time since the 'Big One' when another sizable aftershock hit," Chrisa recalls. "She flew under the house and paced back and forth, afraid to come out."

More than an hour later, the shivering and frightened Pug was finally retrieved.

Now that the shaking has subsided, San Fernando Valley residents like Chrisa and Loris, along with everyone in Southern California, are paying closer attention to preparing for disasters, which includes, for pet owners, keeping current identification tags on all their animals. San Fernando Valley shelters were filled with unidentified dogs and cats, and bulletin boards overflowed with lost pet notices and photographs.

Make sure there's plenty of dog food and water with emergency survival supplies, along with extra leashes and harnesses, and pet, as well as human, first aid kits.

The little "curly tails" have also learned some lessons from the quake. Nobody can say they are anything but inventive and ingenious, even in the most trying of times. I started giving my Pugs treats after each aftershock to calm them. Always on the lookout for opportunities to cadge some extra food, they now run to the treat jar whenever a large truck rumbles by.

CARING STAFF FINDS HOME FOR OL' DOWAGER

By Ranny Green

The Seattle Times Pet Columnist

At the Seattle Animal Control shelter they call her Peg. That's not her real name, but it seems to fit.

It happens every so often at busy shelters, where several thousand dogs are put to death annually, a dog comes along with a special quality — a certain indomitable spirit that overcomes.

"No one here can stand the thought of this dog being put down," says Mary Felix-Klenk, shelter animal-care supervisor. "She has touched the lives of all of us. Maybe it's her will to live. Or that look in her eyes."

The staff has named this charismatic black-tan, silver-muzzled German Shepherd mix Peg (for Peg-a-leg), because she has three legs. She's missing her left rear limb. Like most three-legged counterparts, Peg has managed to overcome this handicap sometimes with reckless abandon.

Apprehended in September, she long ago exceeded the basic 72-hour holding period for strays before euthanasia. While three legs isn't a strike against her, Peg's age — estimated to be between seven and nine years old, and a skin problem, possibly flea allergy dermatitis and/or hypothyroidism, on the lower back — certainly don't enhance her prospects.

"We've been treating the skin problem, and it is improving." says Felix-Klenk. "I'm certain that if someone adopts her and gets her under veterinary care, it can be corrected quickly."

Lisa Hawthorne, a nine-year kennel Animal Control officer, has taken Peg home overnight on numerous occasions, simply to keep her socialized and check out her overall behavior. "Her eyes beckoned, 'I want to go home.'

"She's a marvelous dog. She got along fine with Sunny, my eight-month-old yellow Lab, and with my two cats. Somebody has put some work into this dog. She heels on a leash, loves to ride in the car, comes when called, shakes hands, goes to the door when she needs to go out in the yard to relieve herself, and is protective."

When a stranger came to Hawthorne's door, Peg positioned herself between the door and Peg, cautioning the visitor, "You best not proceed any farther."

"She adapted very quickly to my home," says Hawthorne. "And I'm confident she'd do the same with anyone. Peg has so much love to offer. She'd be great in a single-pet household, but she would meld right in if there are other animals, too."

Hawthorne cited patience, discipline and an ability to readily adapt to new surroundings as Peg's chief virtues. And, oh yes, Peg managed the stairs fine in Hawthorne's two-level home. Aged seven to nine, she'll likely have four to six years remaining.

"It's the quality of life that counts," says Hawthorne, "and I know this dog can offer a family plenty of good times the next few years."

Felix-Klenk adds: "When you go into the kennels, most of the dogs come running up to the gates jumping and barking. I don't blame them, they're just seeking attention. But Peg comes forward, sticks her nose through the bars, has that gleam in her eyes, and her tail wags incessantly."

Make no mistake about it, Peg's a charmer. At our first meeting, she looked me straight in the eyes, bounced over, nuzzled me in the stomach as if saying, "OK, it's my time for a little attention."

At a point when most of our lives are filled with stress — and some with violence — Peg is a prescription for happiness.

Editor's note: Thanks to the extraordinary efforts of Lisa Hawthorne and the staff at Seattle Animal Control this grande dame lives. Peg's strong will and charismatic personality prevailed. Several parties came to the Seattle shelter hoping to adopt her after they read about her plight in Ranny Green's pet column in The Seattle Times. The Chessers were selected.

"I've been in a wheelchair for more than 20 years and Peg has three legs. What a pair, huh?" jokes Mrs. Chesser.

"It's a perfect match," says Lisa. "It's nice to see her go to a good home. A part of me went with her."

CHICO

By Ada P. Wirth

Northern California Keeshond Club Rescue

I was notified by Sacramento County Animal Control that a male Keeshond had come into the kennel and needed to be rescued. He was placed in adoption. No takers. He had developed kennel cough, the deadly condition for a shelter dog. The shelter staff couldn't risk infecting the other dogs. Without breed rescue he would be euthanized.

I hadn't planned on going to the kennel. I had a thousand other things to do, but I went. I visited the dog in the quarantine kennel. I let the shelter staff know I would take him. Keeshonds are very sensitive dogs. He looked so lost. I didn't know what to do with him, but I'd take him. I was very grateful that Animal Control had called. They were very cooperative.

I racked my brain to think of a foster home or somewhere I could place him. I couldn't come up with anyone. Finally, I remembered an elderly woman in Chico, California, about 100 miles northwest of my home. She had recently lost her six-year-old Keeshond to cancer. Her husband was recovering from a stroke. He had adored their dog and was distraught when it died. She had expressed an interest in getting another Kees. Maybe they would be the ones? I knew because of their age and situation they needed a calm dog. Would this year-old dog, and a rescued one at that, work?

Chico, as we now called the dog, demonstrated a calm and loving nature. I called the couple and informed them of the situation. She said she would like to adopt him despite the kennel cough. All right!

Since her car was unreliable, my husband and I headed off the next Saturday morning for Chico. Upon our arrival, the woman greeted us with a big hug. Her husband walked slowly toward us with the help of a special cane. His right side had suffered a paralysis as a result of the stroke. As we approached, he greeted us, a huge grin coming over his face. He grabbed for the dog's leash with his previously paralyzed right hand and took the dog to their porch. He sat down in his wheelchair. Chico proceeded to rest his head on the man's lap.

If only we'd had a video camera to record this joyous moment. It was like they were made for each other. Chico needed this couple, and this couple needed Chico. Rescue, despite the heartbreak, the drain, the expense, does work. The happy placements make it all worthwhile.

ADAM

By M. Suzanne Sims

Mississippi Animal Rescue League volunteer; dog writer; obedience, agility, and tracking trainer; and pet therapy worker

The door opened that day in March many times, as they do in shelters across our country, to admit scores of unwanted animals, many destined to be euthanized. A man carried in a gorgeous tricolored dog weighing about 45 to 50 pounds. When he set the dog on the floor, the dog dropped flat, urinating everywhere, his eyes

huge and filled with fear. I went to the dog to reassure him while another employee took the information. And so it was, Adam and I met when he was only a year old, and March 2, 1993, became his day of rebirth.

The man who brought Adam explained he was a property owner and that his tenants had moved out of state, leaving behind two dogs. Adam was brought to the shelter, but his friend had not survived. At Mississippi Animal Rescue League (MARL), strays are held five days, and I spent those five days working with Adam. Originally, the health technician had no intention of putting him up for adoption, feeling he would have to be one of the ones euthanized. When she saw how much progress he made in just five days, she changed her mind.

I held my breath every time someone seemed interested in him, knowing I wouldn't be able to stand it if he were put to sleep after all he had overcome. One day a woman and her two daughters put a puppy they had been looking at back to adopt Adam, a rare occurrence, so this must be it! Adam stayed to be neutered, but the woman called to say they would not be able to take him.

Spring, being an extremely busy time in shelters, meant Adam's days could still be numbered, but a couple decided to adopt him a while later. They returned him because he tested positive for heartworms, and they said they didn't have the time to see him through the treatment.

As I filed out his "In Ticket," tears rolled down my face. A diagnosis of heartworms means a death sentence at a shelter when so many healthy animals have to be euthanized. Crouching and crying behind the counter, holding Adam, I overheard a woman waiting to adopt an animal ask: "Oh, why did they have to bring him back? Why can't they just treat them?"

Adam had come so far. Why did he have to die. Still crying, I called my vet and learned it would cost $175 to treat a dog his size. As a shelter worker, I knew I could not afford that, but another vet lowered the cost $75, and my boyfriend, Greg, sent the money.

Adam, an active Aussie, had to be crated for four weeks for the treatment. It wasn't easy, but we made it. He and Cinnamon, my first shelter rescue, became instant best friends. The treatment successful, Adam went back up for adoption, this time heartworm-free, basic obedience trained and housebroken.

But, you guessed it. No takers. By this time, four months had passed. In the meantime, I had found a house with a fenced yard. Adam came home with me! Of course, right after I signed the paperwork, five people became interested in Adam. But now he was mine.

Adam earned his CGC only months after our adopting one another, and he is now a certified therapy dog, earning his TDI (Therapy Dogs International) title this past October. I soon realized Adam was an Aussie with tail intact, so in September 1994 I applied for his AKC ILP. After many months and an appeal, I am proud to say Adam is now "ILP'd" and goes by the name MARL's Jumpin' Adam, CGC TDI VCC. MARL is for Mississippi Animal Rescue League, which I chose in the hopes of demonstrating to the public what wonderful pets are at our shelters. VCC is for Versatile Canine Companion, which Adam has recently earned through Clever Canine Companions.

Adam shows remarkable enthusiasm and ability in tracking, agility and obedience work, but he has one area where he shines — therapy work! We began working with the Mississippi Methodist

Rehabilitation Center, and when we walk in all eyes are on Adam and his sister, Cinnamon. We do tricks, demonstrate his article indication skills, and answer questions about dogs, training — you name it. Adam's favorite part of our time there is going to each patient to be petted and loved. One man, reluctant to pet Adam at the beginning of one of our visits was actually hugging him by the end of the session. Adam seems to have the ability to understand these people and their pain.

My time at MARL showed me the need shelters have for devoted volunteers. Adam is a wonderful representative for MARL, as is his brother Harvey, a litter-trained house bunny. Adam is a prime example of what tender love, care, and patience can do for any animal, no matter what their past holds. Anyone can hold the key to their future of promise, love, and happiness. You must, however, be willing to show them the way.

SPIRIT OF ST. NICK

By Danette McLaughlin Grady
Living Free Animal Sanctuary

During the holiday season, one of our employees discovered a dying dog near her home. He had been cruelly shot in the head and front legs with a .22 rifle. When the owner was contacted, he said that he didn't have the money to put the animal to sleep and would just leave him there to die. Living Free Animal Sanctuary went to work immediately. They obtained custody of the dog and rushed him into emergency medical treatment. After hours of surgery, the bullets were removed; unfortunately, so was one eye.

The prognosis was poor, but that was discounting the devotion of the caring staff and the dog's own indomitable spirit. Dubbed "Saint Nicholas" because of his relentless cheerful nature, the courageous fellow struggled to show his appreciation to all who visited him in the shelter clinic. As the months passed, he was showered with love and care (and the occasional forbidden treat), until he was running everywhere, excitedly greeting visitors and trying oh-so-hard to get the administration building cats to play with him.

Nicholas was adopted by Lonnie Thomas, a shelter employee. His playful and friendly personality brings happiness to her constantly, she reports.

BIG MAMA

By Chris Kish
Humane Society of Genesee County, Michigan

We, as shelter employees, want to make certain that people are aware of the tremendous responsibility and honor associated with dog ownership. Success stories, like Big Mama's, make our efforts truly worthwhile.

In early 1995, our cruelty investigators entered a run-down house through a window to rescue Big Mama, a German Shepherd/Mastiff mix, and her puppy. On her own, Mama, an emaciated bundle of skin and bones with nothing but toilet water to drink, was still valiantly trying to care for her puppy. Both received the tender loving care they needed at the shelter, and, as is often the case, the puppy was adopted quickly.

Big Mama eventually found a home too, but her (obviously) fine taste led her to chew on only the most expensive items in her new owners' home! So once again, Big Mama returned to our shelter. The staff, although thrilled to see her, was saddened by the fact that she would once again need to find an owner.

Two months ago, a very kind gentleman happened by her kennel and Big Mama decided that he would be the one. She especially liked the fact that he and his wife owned lakefront property with plenty of room for her to run. We are happy to report that her new family wrote to us to say they were thrilled with Sadie and could not imagine ever giving her away. They included pictures of a 15-

pounds-heavier, healthy, happy Sadie contentedly basking in the sun and running in her yard.

Her family would love to bring her for a visit but fears she will think she has been abandoned once again.

SHELTIE

By John D. Bolton

Although it may be easier to raise a dog from puppyhood, older dogs rescued from whatever source can and do make wonderful pets and companions. It just takes a little time, understanding, patience and lots of love. It seems that the love portion is really the biggest part, and the reward is so fulfilling.

About five years ago, I lost my female Sheltie, Sable, to lymphoma. My male Sheltie, Rogue, and I missed her so much that I contacted a Sheltie rescue group in the Los Angeles area and was told about a black-and-white Sheltie in a terrible situation. Abused, she ended up in the pound where she stayed for more than a year during court battles. Finally, she was released to a shelter rescue organization, which had to move her to at least three foster homes.

When I first met her, she was timid, literally terrified of her own shadow. Her teeth, thanks to puppy mill overbreeding, were in such poor condition that they protruded from her mouth. I don't know what it was about her (especially knowing there would be initial vet bills), but I took her home.

Rogue would have nothing to do with her, nor she with him. All she would do was cower. The vet fixed her teeth, checked her out and determined her to be between five and eight years old. She was a sound dog physically, despite all she'd been through. I worked with her alone and with Rogue. It took a period of time and a lot of love and attention. She became more sure of herself and confident that we were not going to harm her. She blossomed into the Dowager Empress that she is today. Shelties are a special breed. She has just been pure love. Some people thought adopting her was a mistake, but love is a two-way street.

HANNAH

By Jerrie Dean

Provided courtesy of *Animal Press*

My husband, Mark, and I had been married a little over a year when he began hinting about getting a dog. I had had two dogs in my life so far, a beautiful Belgium German Shepherd and a handsome Samoyed. I knew the time and responsibility that was involved with a dog and was not crazy about the idea. Mark began calling places anyway. Before I knew it, I was standing at the door of a blind woman who had called the Basset Hound Rescue Society and reported that she had rescued a Basset Hound.

A Basset Hound. What did I know about a Basset Hound, other than, as my husband put it, they love rabbits and riding around in trucks? When I first saw her, I was a little amazed. Stubby and short, but a body, head, and feet as big as a Retriever, ears that skimmed the floor, and that smell. Nothing matched on her. Her legs were intended for a Dachshund, I'm sure, but her feet were intended for a lion and her ears a giraffe — and that smell, surely a skunk.

When we first met, we did not bond. She snarled at me. But my husband, well, she instantly began to love my husband. The woman told us that her family moved and couldn't take her with them so they left her in the back yard with some food and water. Eventually the barking and howling alerted the neighbors. When they saw the house empty, they knew no one was coming back for her. The woman couldn't bear to listen to the dog howling from abandonment and brought her into her home. She wanted to keep her, but she already had a guide dog.

Both she and Mark looked at me with Basset Hound eyes.

"It's your decision," he stated. Four sets of mournful eyes, one set bloodshot, stared at me. That stinky, stubby, snotty Basset Hound was going home with us, and she knew it.

There was a lot of adjusting for me. She growled at me constantly. She growled when I talked to her or when I came in between her and Mark. I fed her and walked her because I had to, but I didn't love her. How can you get to know her when she growls at you all the time? Could that be it? We just didn't know each other, and we both wanted exclusive attention from Mark. That's silly; she's just a dog.

One evening, when my husband was gone, I knelt down by her. She growled. I looked straight into her eyes and said: "Don't growl at me; I want to love you." Then I began to wrap my arms around her and hug her. What began as a low growl slowly stopped, and a few moments later a sigh, an honest to goodness sigh. I leaned back and her tail began to wag.

"You're a good dog, and I want us all to be a family."

She bowed her head and shoved her forehead into my chest for another hug. She stopped growling at me that day. We began to learn more and more about each other, and I was delighted when I found out she had been trained to bring the leash when she wanted to go for a walk. Nowadays, there aren't too many places she doesn't go to with us. Oh, she used to ride in the back of the truck, but not anymore. Now Hannah rides in the cab with us — right smack in the middle.

SCRUFFY

By Micheal Cronk
San Jose Mercury News

Daisy Wood doesn't hesitate using the word "miracle" when describing how she was reunited with her dog Scruffy.

Wood was convinced her beloved pet was dead. She had identified what she thought was Scruffy's body at the Humane Society of Santa Clara Valley and had the body buried at a pet cemetery in Santa Rosa.

She returned to the humane society a few days later, looking for a new pet in the kennel that houses the male dogs. She found a little dog she liked, but something compelled her to look farther. And there, in the fourth cage down, she saw her Scruffy, a 22-year-old salt-and-pepper Poodle-Terrier mix. Scruffy leaped up and down as he always did when he saw Wood.

"That dog knew his mom, no questions," said humane society staff member Janet Alexander.

The shock was almost too much for Wood, who was recovering from a heart attack.

"I thought it was the beginning of another heart attack," said Wood, a technical writer who lives in Santa Clara. "I dropped my purse and was hanging on the gate trying to remember my breathing exercises. But I knew I had to live to save Scruffy."

Scruffy appeared to be in good health, although his fur was a mess.

"He definitely lived up to his name," said Kay McCleery, the society's director of customer service.

He also hadn't lost any weight. Someone must have been feeding Scruffy because, said Wood, "if he doesn't have his 11 ounces a day, his ribs cave in."

The Scruffy saga began early last August. Wood, 57, went to her heart specialist for a checkup and had a heart attack while on the examining table. She was immediately prepared for surgery and had an angioplasty. After a 10-day hospital stay, she returned home to find that someone had let Scruffy and her other dog, a Brittany Spaniel named Bathsheba, out of the security fence at her home. Bathsheba was soon returned, but Scruffy remained missing. He had no identification tags because Wood had taken his collar off after he caught it on a drawer pull.

Wood began her search in earnest. She filed a lost dog report with the Humane Society of Santa Clara on August 17 and had her daughter draw a sketch of Scruffy that showed his protruding lower canine teeth for posters she placed around Santa Clara. She scoured the society's kennels three or four times a day. She got to know the humane society staff well over the next three weeks.

"People who knew about Scruffy were very supportive," said Wood. "They came up and gave me a hug."

One day, Wood got a call from a person who had seen the poster and said he was sure Scruffy had been picked up, dead, by Animal Services officers. Wood checked with the humane society to see if a dog like Scruffy had been brought in dead. One had. Wood insisted on accompanying Alexander into the freezer to look through the dead animals, which the shelter stores until the bodies can be incinerated.

In the bottom of the third barrel, she found the dog she thought was Scruffy. She was convinced it was Scruffy even though her veterinarian and his receptionist said they didn't think so. She claimed the body and had it buried.

She started looking for another dog at the urging of her vet, children, and heart specialist. "I was crying, crying, crying all the time," said Wood. "My heart doctor said that wasn't good, but I couldn't stop."

That search led her back to Scruffy. After reclaiming Scruffy and taking him to the groomer and the vet, Wood called the pet cemetery where the other dog was buried. She had the tombstone changed. It now reads "Little Stranger."

HARRISON'S STORY

By Linda Love
Pet Orphans Fund

Harrison caused a stir when he arrived at Pet Orphans Fund that Saturday in January. Open house was in progress, and volunteers walked and showed the adoption center's dogs while hopeful "walk-ins" filled the patio and courtyard: gentle Jarrod, a brindle bull Mastiff whose little boys were afraid to play with him; Baron, found on a lawn, legs broken by a car; Roscoe, his throat slashed and left to bleed to death; Spike, a sweet stray who was one dog too many. On this weekend, as has occurred for almost a quarter of a century, good dogs with stories waited to join new families.

No wonder no one noticed the dirty little mass of fur whisked to the groom room, where staff members went into action. Long, matted hair hid everything, including a missing rear leg never formed at birth, but failed to disguise the beauty of his face. And when the cautious clipping and bathing finally ended, Harrison emerged a curly, creamy apricot Terrier mix with button eyes that grew merrier in the weeks ahead. Still, there was that familiar question: How adoptable is this dog?

The call had come two days earlier from the East Valley Shelter, one of the busiest in the Los Angeles city system. Could Pet Orphans save a little three-legged Terrier, 2 1/2-years-old, who had no other chance? Probably given up by his owner, he wasn't protected by

California's law on strays, was granted no period of grace, and would be euthanized. Yes, Pet Orphans would help.

Harrison was neutered and then moved to the adoption center. The suture area from his surgery became infected, and he got an ear infection. Medical treatment began. So did socializing.

He was walked and petted and played with and loved until he became a jaunty little guy who ran like the wind and twirled and held his own unending competition for attention. He was a joy! His shelter medical chart ends with a triumphant April 22 entry, "Healthy."

A month later, Harrison found a home. His new family fell in love with him at first sight. He is pampered and groomed regularly. He is the delight of everyone he meets. Neighbors come by regularly to take him for walks.

One busy day, while a volunteer meeting was in session, a woman walked into the courtyard. A fluffy Dreamsicle of a dog pulling her eagerly to the gathering. People groaned softly — an early walk-in? — and then someone yelled, "Harrison!"

He ran. We ran. He wagged. We petted. He sniffled. The meeting was over. Harrison had stopped the show. Harrison's new mom wanted to come by to say hello and thanks for uniting her with this very special dog. This is what rescue work is all about!

PIPPIN

By Jeanie Robinson-Pownall
from the book *Circle of Compassion,* edited by Elaine Sichel

I found her in the barn. The barn had seen better days; it was tumbledown with gaping holes in the roof that let in the elements. This was actually a good thing because apples fell in through one of the holes and landed in the cow manure. Her chain was four feet long, and by really straining she could reach the apples. She had no collar, and the prongs that attached the clasp to the chain gouged and tore at her neck when she pulled and strained toward the apples. Her neck was raw and rank with infection. I could see there was one apple, tantalizingly out of reach. The blood dripping from her neck showed how hard she had tried to reach it to slake her thirst and hunger.

She greeted me joyously, with the frenzied enthusiasm of a captive greeting her liberator. My heart sank when I smelled the vile mingling of odors: her waste, which she could not quite get out of; the infection of her neck, which dripped pus down her legs and onto the ground; and the cow manure produced from the relatively healthy calf sharing a section of the barn with her.

I had seen thin animals before, but never had I seen a dog this thin. Not only did every rib stand out, but the skin sunk down between each rib. She was a skeleton covered by skin and fur with a pitiful sunken-in face. Yet she had spirit.

As I bent down to examine her neck, I noticed reddish splotches were appearing on my clothing. It was blood, pumped from a gaping wound on her tail. Beneath the blood, white bone glistened.

The veterinarian wasn't sure he could save her — she was emaciated and her neck was gangrenous. Yet her spirit impressed him, as did the trusting brown eyes, huge in her sunken face. "We'll try," was all he would promise.

He tried and so did she, and when I brought her home she sat in front of the couch, directly on my feet, and gently accepted popcorn from my fingers. That night I let her up on the bed; how could I make her sleep on the floor with all those bones poking through her skin? The vet agreed to spay her once she'd doubled her weight. She weighed nineteen pounds when I brought her home from the hospital; she weighed forty-seven pounds in her prime. She always liked apples, and ate my apple cores with relish.

She and I were a pair through the rest of my unmarried years. I kept her impeccably clean and brushed, and enjoyed taking my very friendly, very beautiful, very glossy black dog with the very big feet everywhere with me. I married, had two children, and grew into early middle age while she grew old. During her last year on this earth she saved our two-year-old son's life. On a sub-zero night, while he was headed on his merry way out the front door while the rest of us slept, she positioned herself under our bedroom door and howled. Pretty remarkable, considering she'd been deaf for two years.

After fourteen years of stewardship (she in mine and I in hers), we laid her to rest in the backyard, under the trees where she'd spent much of her twilight years sleeping. The daffodils on her grave bloom every spring, and our children's little sneakered-feet have beaten a path around her resting place. She lived a life that was dominated by good nature, valor, and sweetness. She was adaptable, well-mannered, and got along well with everyone she met. I hope when my time comes I deserve such an epitaph, but I am sure I will fall far short of Pippin.

Pippin was the subject of Jeanie Robinson-Pownall's first cruelty investigation for the Allegheny County SPCA. After her rescue and adoption by the author, she contributed to the organization's educational and fundraising efforts by serving as a mascot and helping staff their informational booth at county fairs and other events.

For Further Reading

How to Teach A New Dog Old Tricks
by Ian Dunbar

Second Hand Dog
by Carol Lea Benjamin

Don't Shoot the Dog
by Karen Pryor

Owners Guide to Better Behavior in Dogs
by Bill Campbell

How to Raise a Puppy You Can Live With
by Rutherford & Neil

Good Owners, Great Dogs
by Brian Kilcommons

The Dog's Mind
by Bruce Fogle

How to be Your Dog's Best Friend
by Monks of New Skete

Positive Dog Training
by Allen Bauman

Coping with Sorrow on the Loss of Your Pet
by Moira Anderson

Active Years for Your Aging Dog
by Hershhorn

Playtraining Your Dog
by Patricia Burnham

Circles of Compassion
A Collection of Humane Words and Works
Edited by Elaine Sichel
1 (707) 823-1306

My Priceless Furs

I'm lucky! I have five fur coats
But not a one I'd wear
For they belong to my five dogs
Whose lives are in my care.

They came to me in different ways
From pounds and puppy mills
Two spent two years of suffering
So man could "cure his ills."

No, I would never wear them
Though freezing cold I'd be.
No, I could never wear them
They don't belong to me.

On winter nights, when temps are low
I'm warm as I can be
Cause my five dogs hop on my bed
And share their coats with me.

—**Florence L Lambert**

Appendix

The Canine Awareness Test©

1. How many dogs are put to sleep every year in the United States?
   - A. 4.7 million
   - B. 6.9 million
   - C. 8.4 million
   - D. 10.6 million
2. What percentage of dogs entering shelters in the United States are euthanized?
   - A. 25%
   - B. 35%
   - C. 45%
   - D. 60%
3. The number one reason dogs are surrendered to shelters is:
   - A. Landlord objects/Moving
   - B. Owner has no time to spend with the dog
   - C. Divorce
   - D. Death of the owner
4. What percentage of dogs remain with their original owners?
   - A. 35%
   - B. 45%
   - C. 60%
   - D. 75%

5. The best time to start training is:
   - A. 12 weeks
   - B. 6 months
   - C. 8 months
   - D. 1 year
   - E. When you get the dog
6. Vaccinations are necessary to protect against serious infectious diseases.

   T F
7. The objective of housetraining is to get the puppy to go on the paper.

   T F
8. Of all dogs obtained, 14% are obtained at shelters.

   T F
9. Shelter dogs need patience and, in most cases, 6 to 12 weeks to adjust to a new home.

   T F
10. If you have a problem with your dog you should live with it.

    T F
11. The most important success factors in obtaining a dog are having a reasonable expectation of the dog's behavior and having the knowledge and confidence to work out any undesirable behaviors.

    T F
12. AKC papers show the dog is bred of high quality.

    T F
13. Spaying/neutering is the most important thing you can do to stop pet overpopulation.

    T F
14. Dogs are independent and like to be alone for long periods of time.

    T F
15. Dogs are happiest living in the back yard.

    T F

16. Dogs enjoy a regular daily routine.
    T F
17. You should feed your dog the same food you eat.
    T F
18. Dogs need to perceive one person in the family as the leader.
    T F
19. It is OK to correct a dog hours after the negative behavior has been committed.
    T F
20. Dogs like to lie around and don't need exercise.
    T F
21. Dogs have feelings.
    T F
22. The best way to train a dog is to use harsh treatment — so they know who is the boss!
    T F
23. How long does it take to train a dog:
    A. 2 weeks
    B. 6 week
    C. 8 weeks for a half-hour daily
    D. Continuously
24. Select the answer that does *not* belong. Crates are a helpful tool in dog care (maximum of 4 hours) and can be used:
    A. To aid in house training.
    B. To prevent chewing and destructive behavior.
    C. To help integrate the dog into the house.
    D. As a safe haven that emulates a den.
    E. As a way to punish your dog

25. Responsible dog ownership means:
    A. Picking up excretion
    B. Not letting the dog bark excessively
    C. Keeping the dog on a leash
    D. Training the dog
    E. Providing regular grooming
    F. Observing all dog laws
    G. Providing daily nourishment, attention and exercise
    H. All of the above

The Canine Awareness Test Answers

1. A 4.7 million, or one every 6.7 seconds

2. D 60%, 15% dogs reclaimed and 25% dogs adopted on average in the United States.

3. A Landlord objects/Moving. The root cause is owners who fail to live up to their commitment and responsibility of dog ownership. All owners should be considerate of their neighbors.

4. A This stems mostly from an owner's inability to deal successfully with behavior problems.

5. E A dog relies on its owner for instruction and care as soon as you take it home.

6. True Dogs need to have defense against fatal diseases.

7. False The object is to get the dog to understand that its place to go is *outside*. The only exception to this is when someone lives in an urban area where walking the dog at night would be hazardous.

8. True There are many, many good dogs in shelters that most people don't consider.

9. True Shelter dogs are kept in kennels and need a period of adjustment to know the rules of the house, feel confident and bond with their owners .

10. False If you experience a problem ask your veterinarian for a referral to a trainer or behaviorist. Most behavior problems can be easily solved with their help.

11. True Know what to expect before a dog comes home.

12. False AKC papers are nothing more than a registration, similar to a birth certificate.

13. True Spaying/neutering will prevent accidental pregnancies and unwanted litters.

14. False Dogs are pack animals and need the company of other people or dogs.

15. False Dogs enjoy the back yard for short duration's but would rather live inside with their owners.

16. True Dogs love routine. The more regularity for feeding, training, excreting and exercise, the better.

17. False Commercial dog foods are specially formulated and nutritionally balanced.

18. False Dogs need to perceive all members of the family as leaders, including children.

19. False Corrections must occur as the behavior is exhibited. You should never hit your dog or use your hands as weapons. This will only teach the dog to fear you. If you do not catch the dog immediately in a negative act, it's too late. Prevent negative behavior from occurring and reinforce positive behavior.

20. False Dogs need daily exercise. A good rule of thumb is twenty-minute walks twice a day.

21. True Dogs miss their owners when they leave, are happy to see them when they come home, can actually mutilate themselves when emotionally distraught and can experience stress and loss of appetite.

22. False The best way to train a dog is by using positive reinforcement methods that emphasize PRAISE.

23. D Training a dog is an ongoing activity. Just as with people.

24. E Crates are a great tool to prevent problems from occurring.

25. H All owners should do their best to make sure their dog is not a problem in the community.

Scoring (Number of Errors)

0-2	Give yourself a treat, you know your dogs.
3-5	Pretty good, with a little brush up your dog would be proud of you.
6+	To properly care for your dog and have a successful relationship it is vitally important that you educate yourself on dog handling and care. Many dogs are abused unknowingly by their owners. Some end up losing their lives. Join an obedience class and educate yourself on canines — the life you save could be your dog's.

The Canine Awareness Test

A Questionnaire for Rescue Individuals Only!

In order to better network with shelters, you should communicate the following information to your area shelter directors:

- How long has your group been doing rescue?
- What is your availability for support to sheltering organizations?
- Do you offer a referral service, physical rescue or advice?
- Do you accept mixes of your breed?
- What do you do with registration papers from rescued animals?
- Can you provide veterinary care for sick or injured purebreds?
- Do you maintain a waiting list of potential adopters?
- What is your screening procedure for placement: personal interview, landlord approval, spay/neuter requirement contract, post adoption follow-up, accept returns, adoption fee (how much), other.
- Do you foster purebreds in your home?

ORDER & REORDER FORM

TO: **CANINE LEARNING CENTERS**
P.O. Box 10515
Napa, California 94581
1 800-354-DOGS (1 800-354-3647)

Enclosed is a check for $________ for ______ copy(ies) of
Choosing a Shelter Dog

_______ Copies @ $12.00 each (1-12 copies) $_______

_______ Copies @ $8.00 each (Minimum 13) $_______

California residents please add 7.25% Sales Tax $_______

Shipping charge: please add $2 for first book and 75¢ for each additional book. 12 or more books **shipped FREE.** $_______

TOTAL $_______

Ship to: ____

Address: ____

City/State/Zip: ______________________________________

Telephone: ____

SPECIAL QUANTITY DISCOUNTS:

Books are available at special discounts for bulk purchases (**12 or more**) for dog-related charitable activities and organizations. Call **CLC Publishing** for information on special quantity discounts.

1 800-354-DOGS

1-800-354-3647

ABOUT THE AUTHOR

Bob Christiansen has devoted his career to improving the relationship between dogs and their families through educational classes, writings and lectures. He co-owns Canine Learning Center, a professional book publishing and dog-training school with ten locations. The school uses gentle, praise-oriented obedience techniques. His school trains approximately 1,000 dogs and their owners yearly.

Through the training school, he has discovered a technique for dog training that successfully integrates the dogs' natural instincts into the human world in which they live. He wrote and published, *Southern California Dog Owners Guide* and *Northern California Dog Owners Guide*, which are regional best sellers.

Christiansen has dedicated himself to helping dogs and their owners achieve the human/animal bond. "I like dogs— mixed breed or purebred, it doesn't matter. I am concerned about their welfare. If more owners understood dog behavior and the need for training, we could reduce the numbers being destroyed by 75%. People are too quick to blame the dog when thing don't go right. Nine times out of ten, it's the owners failure to understand these wonderful creatures."

There is no fundamental difference between man and the higher animals in their mental function.

Charles Darwin

MEDICAL HISTORY / VACCINATION RECORD (Continued)

DATES:	TREATMENT:
	DISTEMPER HEPATITIS LEPTOSPIROSIS PARVOVIRUS PARAINFLUENZA RABIES BORDETELLA LYMES HEARTWORM OTHER
	DISTEMPER HEPATITIS LEPTOSPIROSIS PARVOVIRUS PARAINFLUENZA RABIES BORDETELLA LYMES HEARTWORM OTHER
	DISTEMPER HEPATITIS LEPTOSPIROSIS PARVOVIRUS PARAINFLUENZA RABIES BORDETELLA LYMES HEARTWORM OTHER
	DISTEMPER HEPATITIS LEPTOSPIROSIS PARVOVIRUS PARAINFLUENZA RABIES BORDETELLA LYMES HEARTWORM OTHER
	DISTEMPER HEPATITIS LEPTOSPIROSIS PARVOVIRUS PARAINFLUENZA RABIES BORDETELLA LYMES HEARTWORM OTHER
	DISTEMPER HEPATITIS LEPTOSPIROSIS PARVOVIRUS PARAINFLUENZA RABIES BORDETELLA LYMES HEARTWORM OTHER
	DISTEMPER HEPATITIS LEPTOSPIROSIS PARVOVIRUS PARAINFLUENZA RABIES BORDETELLA LYMES HEARTWORM OTHER
	DISTEMPER HEPATITIS LEPTOSPIROSIS PARVOVIRUS PARAINFLUENZA RABIES BORDETELLA LYMES HEARTWORM OTHER
	DISTEMPER HEPATITIS LEPTOSPIROSIS PARVOVIRUS PARAINFLUENZA RABIES BORDETELLA LYMES HEARTWORM OTHER

IMPORTANT INFORMATION

DOG'S NAME: ________________ Date of Adoption: ___/___/___

Adopted From: ______________________________

Contact: ______________________ Phone: ______________

Breed Type: ______________________ Age: ______ Sex: ______

Color: ________________ Markings: ________________

Veterinary Hospital: ______________________________

Vet's Name: ______________________ Phone: ______________

Emergency Contact: ________________ Phone: ______________

Reason for Relinquishment: ______________________________

HOUSETRAINED?	Y N	OBEDIENCE TRAINED?	Y N
GOOD WITH CHILDREN?	Y N	SPAYED/NEUTERED?	Y N

Trainer/Behaviorist: ________________ Phone: ______________

Comments: ______________________________

____

MEDICAL HISTORY / VACCINATION RECORD

DATES:	TREATMENT:
	DISTEMPER HEPATITIS LEPTOSPIROSIS PARVOVIRUS PARAINFLUENZA RABIES BORDETELLA LYMES HEARTWORM OTHER
	DISTEMPER HEPATITIS LEPTOSPIROSIS PARVOVIRUS PARAINFLUENZA RABIES BORDETELLA LYMES HEARTWORM OTHER
	DISTEMPER HEPATITIS LEPTOSPIROSIS PARVOVIRUS PARAINFLUENZA RABIES BORDETELLA LYMES HEARTWORM OTHER
	DISTEMPER HEPATITIS LEPTOSPIROSIS PARVOVIRUS PARAINFLUENZA RABIES BORDETELLA LYMES HEARTWORM OTHER